Going to Live in Spain

howtobooks

Thank you for buying this book. We hope it will help you to get the most out of living in Spain.

We try to keep our books up to date, but contact details seem to change so quickly that it can be very hard to keep up with them. If you do have any problems contacting an organisation please get in touch, and either we or the author will do what we can to help. And if you do find correct contact details that differ from those in the book, please let us know so that we can put it right when we reprint.

Finally, please give us your feedback so we can go on making books that you want to read. If there's anything you particularly liked about this book – or you have suggestions about how it could be improved in the future – please email us on info@howtobooks.co.uk

Please send for a free copy of the latest catalogue:

How To Books
3 Newtec Place, Magdalen Road,
Oxford OX4 1RE, United Kingdom
email: info@howtobooks.co.uk
http://www.howtobooks.co.uk

The Daily Telegraph

Going to Live in Spain

*A practical guide to enjoying
a new lifestyle in the sun*

HARRY KING

howtobooks

First published by
How To Books Ltd, 3 Newtec Place
Magdalen Road, Oxford OX4 1RE. United Kingdom.
Tel: (01865) 793806. Fax: (01865) 248780.
email: info@howtobooks.co.uk
http://www.howtobooks.co.uk

First edition 2003
Reprinted 2003
Reprinted 2005

British Library Cataloguing in Publication Data
A catalogue record for this book is available from the British
Library

Cover design by Baseline Arts Ltd, Oxford
Produced for How To Books by Deer Park Productions,
Tavistock
Typeset by PDQ Typesetting, Newcastle-under-Lyme, Staffs.
Printed and bound by Cromwell Press, Trowbridge, Wiltshire.

NOTE: The material contained in this book is set out in good
faith for general guidance and no liability can be accepted
for loss or expense incurred as a result of relying in particular
circumstances on statements made in the book. The laws and
regulations are complex and liable to change, and readers should
check the current position with the relevant authorities before
making personal arrangements.

Contents

Preface

Spain – so many things to do and so many places to see. There is the cordiality of the people, the incomparable scenery, the beaches of fine sand, the days of sunshine, the high mountains, the vast plains, the nightlife, the evenings, the magnificent cuisine, the restaurants.

Too many hours or too many pages are necessary to say what Spain has to offer. There is only one way to be sure: come and see it for yourself. Coming to Spain to work, for a long-term stay or for retirement can be a step into the unknown. But if some simple preparation is undertaken it can be a step into sunshine and happiness.

Apart from those following a career, why do people move to Spain? Well usually the family has grown up and left home, so for the first time people are free to decide how to spend the rest of their lives. Getting to know another country and its culture is an attractive idea, and so is saying goodbye to cold winters. Perhaps more important is a feeling of not wishing to continue for the rest of one's life doing exactly the same thing. A desire to broaden horizons, to see new places, to meet new people, to enjoy new hobbies, to have a challenge are all the ingredients for a new lifestyle.

Many thousands of British, German and Scandinavian couples move for these reasons. Over the years they have holidayed in their thousands in Spain, enjoying the country, the people and the climate. It is still a relatively cheap country where one can enjoy a standard of living that is just not possible in any Northern European country. It is close to home. Travelling by air, rail and sea or by using the Channel Tunnel can be quick and it can be cheap. Keeping in touch is easier and visits by friends more likely.

Permanent residence is not just a continuous holiday. It starts with a honeymoon period, going to many parties and making new friends. Of course this does not last. But there is no returning home; there is no office, no salary and no pressure. It is important not to get bored. *Cerveza* drinking and sun worshipping can take its toll. Keep active by working part time in a non-demanding situation, or by joining several social clubs and partaking in the many sporting activities available. Have a full and busy life, do the things you enjoy, keep happy, healthy and feel young.

Of course there are some problems. Charming people as they are, the Spaniards do tend to speak very rapidly in a regional language which seems to be quite different to the Spanish learned at night school back home. They have a different body clock too. They can be noisy. Then there are the frustrating delays. People do not rush about. If you need something repaired, it often takes longer than it should. But one adjusts and learns to be patient.

Today's Spain is a young vibrant country barely three decades old. Tourism has changed its face forever. Fishing villages have been replaced with skyscraper hotel blocks. It now has a rapidly expanding economy reaping the benefits of membership of the EU. Major international companies are investing in the country against a background of stable political government and a multilingual labour force.

Yet only a few kilometres inland villages, towns and cities lie untouched retaining their own distinctive lifestyle. The old links to agriculture still exist. Orange and lemon groves, almond trees, thousands of acres of vines and millions of olive trees still remain.

The aim of this book is to help you get the most out of living in Spain, to impart knowledge on how to deal with problems and to give information on how to enjoy life. Lots of people have now spent many years here and if they were still living elsewhere would not hesitate to make the same decision again. They feel Spain is now home. They have been revitalised, enjoy a different lifestyle and feel young again.

Harry King
Pedreguer
Spain

Acknowledgements

I am grateful for the information supplied by Dr Tony Warnes at Sheffield University. His paper on the international dispersion of pensioners from affluent countries is the only real study on retirement locations. The interpretation, summary and any inaccuracy are mine alone.

In a second-hand shop in Javea some manuscripts came to light from pioneering ex-pats of 25 years ago. The problems were similar to today's, but hotels, tourists and the euro have changed things a bit. One theme came through – the humour and ability of people in a new environment to win through. Garry Marvin unwittingly, partly, set the framework for this book and in particular the colour of the bullfight.

Quintin Jardine's comic masterpiece about Dali was an inspiration. The BBC historical records were reassuringly accurate and although the Spanish Tourist Board supplied much information, little was used.

Lastly once again I would like to thank my partner Joan Stock for her support, contribution and checking the final manuscript for facts, omissions and errors.

$$\left(1 \right)$$

A Backdrop to the Country

FACTS, FACTS AND MORE FACTS

Reino de España – the Kingdom of Spain

Mainland Spain covers an area of half a million square kilometres and has a coastline of 2,100 kilometres. Spain includes both the Canary and Balearic Islands, administers two small enclaves in Morocco known as Ceuta and Melilla and three island groups near Africa. The British dependency of Gibraltar is situated at Spain's southern extremity.

It is a big country and the second largest in Europe after France. The interior of Spain is a vast plateau called the Meseta bound to the north-east by the Pyrenees, in the south-west by the Sierra Morena and in the south by the best-known Sierra Nevada. Across the Meseta itself many rivers have cut deep valleys. Much of the coastline is steep and rocky but there is a narrow costal plain bordering the Mediterranean.

The highest point is Pico de Tiede on Tenerife at 3,718 metres above sea level. The Meseta makes Spain the highest, most mountainous area of Europe.

Population

The population of 40 million is less than many European

countries. With 78 people per square kilometre it is one of the lowest population densities in Europe. Spain, despite being 97% a Catholic country, has a low birth rate and a high life expectancy of 75 years for men and 80 years for women. Many Spaniards are now urban dwellers. Madrid, the capital, has the largest conurbation. A million British now live in Spain concentrated in the capital, Barcelona, the Costas and the Islands.

Language

Castellano Spanish is the romance language of the country. *Catalán*, modified French, is spoken in the north east. Valenciano, Basque and Galician are other, difficult to understand, regional dialects. Two hundred million people speak Spanish worldwide, mainly in the former Spanish Empire, making it the third most popular language after English and Chinese. English is the business language in Madrid and Barcelona. It is well understood in the Costas and Islands, but is rarely spoken or understood in rural areas.

Main cities

The principal cities are Madrid, situated in the geographical centre of mainland Spain, being the seat of central government and an important commercial centre, quickly followed by Barcelona, a commercial and industrial city with a large port. There is an intense rivalry between the two cities, both political and sporting. Valencia, the third largest city which faces the Mediterranean, is an important area for car manufacturing. Seville, the fourth largest city located in the south-west exports agricultural produce such as olive oil, fruit and wine.

Bilbao on the northern coast is a modern port. Saragossa is another important industrial centre.

Economy

The main agricultural products are barley, wheat, sugar beet, vegetables, citrus fruits, wine and olive oil. The largest fishing catches are tuna, sardines, mussels, squid and octopus. There are coal and iron ore mines. Manufacturing comprises motor vehicles, machinery, ships and boats, chemicals, steel, textiles and footwear.

The main exports are cars, machinery, fruit and vegetable produce, iron ore and textiles. Imports consist of fuels and petrol, machinery, electrical equipment, vehicles, chemicals and food products. Spain's major trading partners are France, Germany, Italy, the UK, the USA and Portugal.

The economy is, however, changing from a tradition of agriculture to that of a semi-industrial nation, although it still has the largest fishing fleet in Europe with a poor reputation of being widely suspected of flouting EU regulations, quotas and net sizes. Ten per cent of the workforce is engaged in tourism with a further 10% in agriculture and 1% in fishing. Encouraged by EU grants, industry is expanding rapidly, the erection of new colourful buildings clearly visible alongside busy main roads. There is a huge, duplicated civil service.

Unemployment is 8.5%. Although high by some European standards, the current level of unemployment is the lowest since 1979. The unemployment rate for women is two and a half times the rate for men.

The Monarchy

The King of Spain is Juan Carlos I. The Royal family have a palace in Madrid and another in Mallorca. The Spanish monarchy was restored in 1975. Although Franco nominated Juan Carlos as his heir this blessing was initially regarded as being a tarred brush. However, he energetically supported the transition to democracy. During 1981 the long simmering resentment in military circles against rapid change resulted in an attempted coup to seize power. King Carlos narrowly foiled the coup by convincing most of the military units to remain loyal to the government and his courageous opposition to the attempted coup made him a hero.

In an age when deference has gone out of fashion and the ruled can pass qualified judgement on the rulers, the monarchies of Europe struggle for an identity. Too big, not in touch, too expensive, old fashioned – such cries are only quieted at periods of national significance or private loss.

No such problem exists for *El Rey* (the King) of Spain.

GOVERNING MODERN SPAIN

In 1978, Spain adopted a new constitution which restored the identity of ancient kingdoms and regions originally making up the nation in 1492. The result was a kind of United States of Spain. It is now a tightly regulated country having five levels of government. The top two levels comprise a congress and senate of elected representatives from the provinces, the islands and the regions. There are 17 autonomous regions, called *comunidades*, with their own parliaments and governments. This has led to a massive duplication of bureaucracy, because in addition to its own parliament each *comunidade* also has separate representation from the state. The autonomous regions are further divided into *provincias* and then into the smaller *municipios*.

To the ordinary Spaniard politics start and stop at the *ayuntamiento* (the town hall). Situated in the *Plaza Mayor* of each village, town or city the building is bedecked with flags of the *comunidad*, the country and Europe, signifying its importance as the focus of everyday life. The town hall is the home of the *municipio*, a council headed by a mayor and a number of councillors all of whom are elected. It is responsible for keeping the streets clean, collecting garbage, street lighting, water supply and sewerage, roads, cemeteries, schools, planning, traffic control, parks, libraries, markets, social services, fire prevention and public sports facilities. It is at the town hall where some taxes are paid, where licences are issued, where the right to vote is granted and where births and deaths are recorded.

Four Prime Ministers have held power since the restoration of democracy – Suarez, Gonzalez, Aznar and Zapatero. Suarez managed the transition of the country well during the formative years of democracy consulting with all the major political groups to arrive at a consensus approach. Gonzalez steered the country to remain within NATO and to obtain membership of the EU in 1986. More importantly he ensured Spain played a dynamic role in European affairs and encouraged Spain's culture to blossom in numerous fields giving rise to the nation's increased self-confidence. Aznar tackled the budget deficit provoking some discontent with resultant strikes but maintaining the country's strong economic ties with Europe. In the last decade a concentration of political activity has focused on improving Spain's economic growth. Then in 2004 the Madrid train bombings occurred. Terrorism had come to Spain. Zapatero bowed to pacifist pressures.

Spain maintains a well-equipped armed service. Women are accepted into all branches. The government has close defence ties with the United States which has maintained naval and air bases in Spain.

Although the country has transformed itself into a tolerant, democratic society it is still trying to shake off the shackles of the era when heavyweight bureaucracy ruled the day. Great strides have been made but there is still a long way to go as the decentralised government battles with duplication of effort and unnecessary bureaucracy.

Internally it is still troubled by the Basque separatist group called ETA (Euzkadi ta Azkatasuna – 'Basque homeland and liberty'). Now that ETA is officially classed as a terrorist organisation there seems to be the political will in Madrid to deal with the problem. Since 1968 over 800 people have been murdered by ETA – mostly high-profile public citizens.

In 1999 border controls into Gibraltar were tightened in

order to put pressure on the British government over its stance on sovereignty. No one doubts that the role of this enclave is largely historic and its people are set in their ways. But it is easy to forget that Spain too has similar enclaves in Morocco and steadfastly refuses to hand them back to that country.

The economy is booming. A new motorway network has opened up the country. The pace of change is dramatic, purposeful and peaceful. Its people, so long oppressed, are now vibrant, confident, open, tolerant and justifiably proud of their achievements. With the Olympic Games, European Games and Expo Exhibitions all being held in Spain in the last decade the world is seeing it competing and winning at an international level.

PROS AND CONS OF LIFE IN SPAIN

Cost of living

Spain is no longer the cheap and cheerful country it once was. The cost of living has increased considerably over the last decade. However, with the exception of the large cities, the cost of living is still lower in coastal and rural areas than it is in the United Kingdom, Ireland, Germany and France. It is significantly lower than the cost of living in the Scandinavian countries and is on a par with Florida.

Spain's location too affects the cost of living. There is an abundance of locally produced food and wine, not only fresh from the market garden of Europe, but also cheap and plentiful. It is truly amazing the beneficial effect of sunshine on day-to-day living costs. Sure, utility bill unit costs for water, electric, gas and telephone may be slightly high, but they are under government scrutiny and sometimes reduce. Thus, overall, the total cost of living package is very much cheaper than its Northern European equivalent.

Something for everyone
There is more to life in Spain than the Costas. Only a few miles inland, traditional unspoilt Spain opens up. The transformation is remarkable as high-rise modern buildings, set in equally clean cities, are quickly left behind to be replaced by small white-walled villages and then, even further inland, by individual white houses scattered over the hillsides.

There is a clever tourist poster of Andalucia that emphasises the diversity that Spain offers. It starts at the top with blue sky and sun, slightly lower down it has skiers on the snow capped Sierra Nevada, in the middle drawings of Moorish Granada, Seville, and Córdoba, near the bottom flamenco and bullfighting, and at the bottom the tourist resorts of Marbella, Málaga and Torremolinos facing a beach and the Mediterranean Sea. There really is something for everyone in Spain.

Medical facilities
Medical and dental facilities are among the best in Europe. There are many new hospitals staffed by highly qualified doctors and nurses. A high percentage of the cost of this service is provided from private resources. In addition to the local doctor's surgery, the chemist occupies a unique position in the medical hierarchy by providing remedies for simple ailments.

Crime

Spain does have a high petty crime rate. Homes have to be protected by security grills on doors and windows. Cash, passports and electrical goods are the main targets. The theft of motor scooters is so high that insurance companies do not accept this risk. The police seem unable to reduce these incidents necessitating citizens to ensure protection of their own person and property.

Pickpockets, operating in gangs, are active at all open-air markets, indoor markets and within some supermarkets, particularly when thronged with people during the busy summer season.

It is wrong to point the finger at any nationality, social or occupational group because this is the result of increased prosperity within a tolerant society. While murder, bank robbery and crimes of passion are reported in the popular press these are a rarity. As long as sensible precautions are taken, the streets of Spain are safe for both adults and children.

Red tape

Unfortunately Spain is a nation of bureaucrats. Red tape stifles simple daily transactions and frustrates all nation-alities, including the Spaniards themselves. It is very difficult to deal with, most people opting out of the cycle by employing their own personal 'red-tape-cutter' known as a *gestor* (see Chapter 12).

Mañana

The last major downside of Spain is its cultural feature called *mañana* – never do something today if it can be put off to tomorrow, or the day after, or perhaps never to be done at all. To live successfully in Spain it is necessary to come to terms with its culture. Coping with *mañana* is a necessary skill that just has to be acquired. It is best seen with builders, repairmen or when a car breaks down, or indeed any occurrence requiring a commitment to a time or date. A shrug of the shoulders, an upturned hand, a slight bow of the head, a moment of silence is *mañana* in progress. Do not fight it, as no single person can change the culture of a nation. No matter how difficult, learn to live with it.

Mañana does not apply to services such as trains, buses or planes. It is also said that the only thing that starts on time in Spain is a bullfight.

THE BIG NUMBER ONE – CLIMATE
Hardly surprisingly the overwhelming attraction of Spain is its excellent climate. It has a large landmass, with extensive high plateaus and mountain ranges. The influence of the Mediterranean and Atlantic produces a wide range of climatic conditions. Summers everywhere are hot. In winter the north is the wettest, the Costas and the Islands mild, and surprisingly the interior can drop below freezing (see Figure 1).

Some parts of the Costa Blanca have been described by the World Health Federation as having one of the healthiest climates in the world, a fact not lost when promoting features of the area.

Region	Northern Spain				Catalonia				Costa Blanca			
Season	Spr	Sum	Aut	Win	Spr	Sum	Aut	Win	Spr	Sum	Aut	Win
Max temp (°C)	25	36	25	15	27	37	27	27	27	36	29	22
Min temp (°C)	1	9	2	−7	3	13	2	−5	6	16	9	1
Sunshine daily (hrs)	6	9	5	2	8	11	6	4	8	11	7	6
Monthly rain (mm)	83	46	107	120	46	24	30	22	40	5	52	30

Region	Costa del Sol				Balearics				Canaries			
Season	Spr	Sum	Aut	Win	Spr	Sum	Aut	Win	Spr	Sum	Aut	Win
Max temp (°C)	28	41	30	18	23	33	26	18	26	32	30	25
Min temp (°C)	9	18	11	4	6	16	8	2	11	17	15	10
Sunshine daily (hrs)	8	11	7	6	7	11	6	5	7	9	7	7
Monthly rain (mm)	46	0	64	61	32	3	77	39	13	0	28	36

Figure 1. Temperature profile

Climate has to be a balance – not too hot, not too cold, a little bit of rain to grow the crops but not too much to deter people, some snow in the mountains for recreational purposes but not enough to affect communications. Northern Spain has its lush green pastures. The Costas offer sun and sand coupled with the clear blue waters of the Mediterranean. The southern rolling hills of Andalusia attract little movement in the blistering summer heat. The Balearic and Canary Islands are always pleasant. Madrid, the capital, is either freezing or roasting. Córdoba in the South is noted as the 'frying pan' of Europe.

The Mediterranean region has the best climatic balance:

◆ 320 days of sunshine per year;

◆ 11.5 hours of sunshine per day in summer;

◆ 14 inches of rain per year;

◆ average spring temperature 7 to 27 degrees centigrade;

◆ average summer temperature 17 to 36 degrees centigrade;

◆ average autumn temperature 9 to 30 degrees centigrade;

◆ average winter temperature 1 to 23 degrees centigrade.

While Northern Europe is being deluged with rain and battered by wind with roads closed by snow and ice affecting transport, you can almost guarantee that Alicante and Málaga will be bathed in sunshine. But not all of Spain enjoys a Mediterranean climate. Here are some less attractive variations:

◆ San Sebastian – 41 inches of rain per year;

◆ Madrid – average lowest winter temperature: minus 5 degrees centigrade;

◆ extremadura – average highest summer temperature: 41 degrees centigrade.

While there may be other reasons for coming to Spain, climate is the big, big number one. It is healthy, makes one feel good and equally important keeps the heating bills and domestic costs low.

DID YOU KNOW?
Rain and snow

Despite Spain's excellent climate, things occasionally go wrong. When rain falls it can be heavy and prolonged. The water runs off the baked, hard soil into dry riverbeds and finally out to sea. As there are very few drains, flooding of roads frequently occurs. The following is an extract from a newspaper in April 2002:

> Emergency services from Castellon to Almeria have been placed on red alert this weekend after meteorologists forecast similar torrential downpours and gale force winds to those that caused millions of Euros worth of damage on Tuesday when flash floods claimed two lives.
>
> Downpours of up to 300 litres per square metre fell in Javea, Gata and Pedreguer. Floods in Javea left the area completely isolated by road. About 100,000 people were without electricity for eight hours as rainwater flooded the electricity station. A four-storey building in Alcoy collapsed due to the torrential rain and high winds.

In Southern Spain the phenomenon of 'Sahara rain' occurs once or twice per year. Rain clouds moving north from the Sahara desert deposit a thick red dust on clean white houses. This disconcerting act of nature necessitates a major clean-up with brushes, water and power hoses.

High in the mountains of the Costa Blanca exist many well-preserved snow wells or *neveras*. They were built in strategic locations, where snow drifted in dips or hollows. They were dug deep into the ground, lined with stone, had a number of access doors and a conical roof to ward off sunlight. Stone steps or iron rungs enabled the pressers and block cutters to reach the bottom. The size and solid construction of the *neveras* are truly amazing.

Before the days of the refrigerator snow was commercially harvested, compacted into a well and left until summer when it was cut into blocks of ice. In the cool of the night the ice was carried down the mountains by mule, donkey and cart to the distant centres of population. It was an active industry, but where is the snow today? There is none. Can this be global warming?

It does not end here as elsewhere, deserted mills, obviously powered by water now lie along side a dry riverbed. Where has the water gone?

SUMMARY

+ The Kingdom of Spain is the second largest country in Europe after France. It has 40 million inhabitants.

+ The economy is changing to that of an industrialised nation. Traditional agriculture is in decline.

+ The last 30 years have seen Spain emerge from a bloody civil war to a strong democracy playing an important role in Europe.

+ The devolved autonomy is rather like a United States of Spain. It has a strong monarchy.

+ The *ayuntamiento* (town hall) is an important focal point for everyday life.

+ The cost of living is cheaper in Spain than in many northern European countries.

◆ There is something for everyone in Spain. Medical facilities are good.

◆ Petty crime, red tape and the infuriating attitude of *mañana* are a few of the downsides.

◆ The excellent climate is Spain's number one asset. But when it rains, it isn't only on the plain.

(2)

Milestones, Markers
and the Arts

A milestone is defined as an important event or a turning point in history. There are three important milestones in the history of Spain. One is the impact of Moorish invaders, another is the period when Spain ruled the world and the last was the Franco era.

Markers identify Spain's stunning national parks and its varied farming. The artistic side of Spain is distinguished by its architecture, painters and writers.

THE HERITAGE OF THE MOORS

Arab invaders from northern Africa in AD 711 produced a new society, which combined three distinct ethnic and religious groups. Muslims now joined Christians and Jews. These Muslim settlers were known as 'The Moors'. A powerful presence was established in Andalusia where mathematics, science and architecture flourished. Competent administrators, they also brought new crops such as rice and oranges to Spain.

Córdoba was to be the great shining light of the Islamic culture. In time, it became a centre of learning, literature, and the arts. The Arabic numerals enabled the Spanish Moors to invent algebra. Great libraries sprang into being, with the one at Córdoba containing 250,000 books. Poetry flourished together with fine art, silken garments, elaborate glassware and pottery. Moorish surgeons used full anaesthetics to carry out brain surgery and eye operations, so that rich people from all over Europe used their services. Above all, the Moors built great mosques and palaces. The great Mosque in Córdoba and the mighty Alhambra in Granada bear witness to the magnificence of Moorish architecture.

The Moorish legacy to modern Spain is immense. Over 4,000 words of modern Spanish are of Arabic origin. The elaborate courtesy of many Spanish phrases reflects Islamic greetings. Spain's most impressive buildings, palaces and castles are Moorish. Many words used in the context of architecture, mathematics and the practice of medicine are traceable to Arabic. The wild dances that evolved into the Flamenco came from Africa. Alone among European nations Spain will always echo its North African past.

One other group was to have their lives profoundly affected by the centuries of Moorish occupation. The Jews of Spain enjoyed, for the first and last time in their troubled history, a respected role in daily life. Freed from persecution they were highly valued as merchants, administrators, ambassadors and financiers. As a group in the Christian Moorish world of Spain, both sides trusted them. Córdoba attracted Jewish scholars from all over Europe. Salamanca created a school of translation at the famous University, where Jewish, Christian and Moorish scholars worked side by side, translating the Holy Books of all three religions into Spanish.

Although Moors established themselves in the south their power stretched to every corner of the peninsula. However, Christian kingdoms flourished in the far north and were eventually responsible for a rebellion that became known as the Reconquest. It took Christian troops seven centuries to achieve a definite end to Muslim rule in Spain, a so-called triumph that continues to be celebrated to this day by a fiesta known as 'The Moors and Christians'.

The expulsion of the cultured Moors and the rich industrious Jews left great gaps in the agricultural and administrative expertise of Spain. The Moors had also been responsible for the intricate terraces and irrigation systems that had created exotic gardens and fruitful fields of orchards that still exist today, and the Jews had been highly placed in court circles as advisers. Without the Moors and the Jews, Spain suffered from a decline in agriculture and the judiciary.

CONQUERING THE WORLD

Christopher Columbus was a national hero. He persistently proposed to the Catholic government voyages to the New World. The thought of riches led them to sponsor Columbus as the monarchs were short of funds.

His first voyage in 1492 was a modest affair comprising three ships and a total crew of 90. With the crew on the point of mutiny he landed in the Bahamas and later discovered Cuba and the Dominican Republic. Buoyed by success the second voyage a year later was a grand affair comprising 17 ships and 1,500 crew. It lasted three years and discovered countless West Indian islands. The natives were, however, rebellious, and fighting was common. Five shiploads of natives were sent back to Spain – a start of the slave trade.

The third voyage from Cádiz in 1498 was a failure. Columbus thought he had discovered South America but in actual fact it was only Venezuela. He failed to find the passage westward to the Pacific. Politics within the monarchy ensured Columbus returned in irons. There was a fourth voyage. But Columbus was now a nuisance. The three ships searched vainly for the westward passage.

Columbus was a brilliant navigator and had a natural instinct for the stars, the sky and the wind. He had an obsession to prove that his ideas about a westward passage were correct. Although he was wrong this does not minimise his achievements for it was Columbus who introduced the Old World to the New World.

Soon after Columbus's discovery of the Bahamas, the Spanish invaded Central and South America, conquering Mexico, Peru and Chile. In doing so they destroyed many civilisations. The Spanish conquerors stood open mouthed when they first saw the capital city of the Aztecs, but when the conquest ended in 1521 they had destroyed the native city and built in its place what was to become Mexico City.

In the sixteenth century, vast quantities of gold and silver flowed across the Atlantic to Spain. Not only did Spain profit from the precious metals brought back from the

Americas, but also from an amazing range of new crops. Potatoes, tomatoes and maize were introduced. Tobacco, spices and cacao were discovered.

Spain's most productive era, known as the Golden Age, was a time of great achievement. This brilliance occurred, however, against a background of economic deterioration and ruinous wars with the Low Countries and France. Spain gradually lost its influence in Europe. The 133-ship Armada suffered a further major defeat when it attempted to invade England as the Spanish galleon, although sturdily built, was hard to manoeuvre and was no match for swifter vessels.

THE FRANCO ERA

In July 1936 a military revolt against the government took place. The country was soon divided between the rebel-led Nationalists located generally in the agricultural areas led by General Franco and the Republicans located in the industrialised areas. A three-year civil war ensued.

Both sides received help from abroad. Fascist Italy and Nazi Germany sent troops, arms and aircraft to aid the Nationalists. The USSR sent military equipment and advisers to the Republican loyalists who were also aided by idealistic volunteers from Europe and America.

The Nationalists won after three years. The savage war was followed by a vindictive peace. Franco made no attempt at national reconciliation. Hundreds of thousands of people were imprisoned and 37,000 executed during the four years after the war. The main political forces during this period were the Army and, surprisingly, the Church which had developed close ties with Franco.

What role did the UK play? Officially it was neutral, but murky dealings have since come to light. Franco was commanding the Canary Islands garrison when the right-wing military coup against the Spanish republic was launched. He was ferried to take command of the military revolt in a British De Havilland Dragon Rapid aircraft chartered from Olley Air Services at Croydon aerodrome and flown by Captain Cecil Bebb.

That much has been known for some time, but recently declassified documents at the Public Record Office at Kew, England show a far deeper involvement. On the plane with Franco was Major Hugh Pollard who was an experienced intelligence officer who later, in 1940, was stationed in Madrid working for MI6. Pollard spoke Spanish, and was a firearms expert who had served in wars and revolutions in Ireland, Mexico and Morocco. Since Special Branch at Croydon monitored all international flights at that time they must have had knowledge of its purpose, which ultimately was to help to overthrow a democratically elected government.

At the end of the Second World War, Spain was an international outcast. The UN ostracised the Franco regime and many countries cut off diplomatic ties. But with the outbreak of the Korean War in 1950 Franco was seen as an important ally against communism and a slow re-emergence took place in the next decade as Spain attempted to integrate itself into the world economy.

From 1961 the economy boomed because of rapid industrial growth and a substantial rise in tourism. Owing to a labour shortage, wages increased, trade unions developed, and agriculture was mechanised. Greater prosperity brought rapid social change. There was massive migration from rural to urban areas bringing in its wake a government-sponsored housing programme. During this period, social pressures brought a change from an oppressive rule to one more liberal.

The last few years of Franco's regime were characterised by increasing prosperity, greater liberalisation but equally greater social unrest. Strikes and demonstrations were commonplace. ETA in the Basque country continued their cycle of violence and counter-violence in an attempt to gain independence. The restoration of democracy took place upon the succession of King Juan Carlos following the death of Franco in 1975.

The new democratic constitution was enthusiastically accepted by most sections of society but the Basque Provinces still resented being tied to Spain and supported ETA. Similarly the Catalans pushed for greater control over local affairs and demanded greater language rights. The Galician's too distanced themselves from Madrid. All this led to creating a Spain of 'autonomous communities', the broad format of the government of today.

STUNNING NATIONAL PARKS

Few countries in Western Europe have such unspoiled scenery as Spain. More than 200 nature reserves protect a broad range of ecosystems. The most important areas are the 11 national parks, the first of which was established in 1918.

Mountains

Some of Spain's finest scenery is to be found in the two national parks in the north where rivers have carved stupendous gorges between the high mountain peaks.

The National Park of the Picos is now Europe's largest national park straddling the three regions of Asturias, Cantabria and Castilla y León. In some parts, deep gorges cut through the rocks. Elsewhere green valleys support dairy farming. The Picos offer superb hiking, rock climbing and caving.

The National Park of Ordessa y Monte Perdido, situated in the high Pyrenees, is accessible only on foot. In autumn and winter, snow makes it inaccessible to all, except those with specialist climbing equipment. In the high summer many way marked trails can be tackled by the reasonably fit. But Pyrenean weather can change quickly. In case of need there are several *refugios* providing basic food and shelter.

Wetlands

The wetlands, including coastal strips and freshwater marshes, are ever-changing environments. Seasonal floods rejuvenate the water providing nutrients for animal and plant growth. These areas are rich feeding grounds for birds.

The national park of Donana covers in excess of 185,000 acres. It is a massive wetland of marshes and sand dunes.

As the land is not suitable for human settlers wildlife is able to flourish. In 1969, this large area became the protected home to threatened species and thousands of migratory birds.

Volcanic landscapes

Three very different parks protect parts of the Canary Islands' amazing volcanic scenery.

- Caldera de Taburiente on La Palma is a volcanic crater surrounded by woods.

- Mount Teide in Tenerife, a high mountain usually covered in snow, has unique alpine flora.

- Lanzarote's Timanfaya is composed of barren but atmospheric lava fields.

Islands

Cabrera, off the coast of Mallorca, is home to rare plants, reptiles and seabirds. The surrounding waters are important for their marine life.

DIVERSE FARMING

Almonds, oranges and olives are the characteristic signature of rural Spain but its varied climate has created a much wider range of crops.

Land can be broadly divided into dry land used for olives, wheat and vines, and irrigated land planted with citrus trees, rice and vegetables. Much of the farmland on the vast open plains of central Spain is covered in wheat. The high rainfall and mild summers of northern Spain make it suitable for dairy farming. Oranges, lemons and clementines are grown on the coastal plains beside the Mediterranean. Olive trees are planted in long, straight lines on the rolling hills of Andalusia. Almeria hosts acres and acres of plastic sheeting covering vegetable and soft fruit crops, making it the market garden of Europe. Vast quantities of wine are produced in Spain (see Chapter 10).

What of traditional crops? Sweet oranges are grown in dense, well-irrigated groves on the virtually frost-free coastal areas close to Valencia. The sweet smell of orange blossom in springtime is unmistakable. Trees of the bitter orange are often planted for shade and decoration in parks and gardens. Almonds grow on dry hillsides in many parts of Spain. Cherries grow too, the spring blossom being spectacular. Olive trees grow slowly, living to a grand old age, the olive being harvested during the winter months and pickled for eating or pressed for oil.

Several other crops exist. Tropical species, such as avocado have been introduced, and bananas are a major crop of the Canary Islands. Elsewhere, peaches and loquats are grown commercially.

DID YOU KNOW?
The cork tree

Cork is best known as a stopper in wine bottles. It allows the wine to mature in the bottle. Where does the cork come from? Answer, from the evergreen cork oak tree, which grows in the south of Spain. Of course cork is used in other products such as floor tiles, insulation and gasket seals but try telling that to a red wine drinking Spaniard.

Growing to a height of 15 metres the cork oak lives for 600 years. It takes 20 years for the first bark to appear and when cut a further seven years to regenerate. When the cylinders of cork are cut off with axes the tree immediately starts to bleed resin protecting it until the new bark grows. The cut cork bark is left in the sun for a year then boiled to soften it prior to processing at a factory.

DISTINCTIVE ARCHITECTURE

The *Plaza Mayor*

Almost every town in Spain has its main square, the *plaza mayor*. It acts as a focus for local life. A church, the town hall, shops and bars usually overlook it. Seats are placed around the edges. It is a home to cultural events.

The *Ermita*

Almost everywhere there exist white painted *ermitas*, isolated chapels or shrines dedicated to the local saint. In villages and towns they will be a focal point for religious events and processions throughout the year. They are situated on high ground overlooking the town, are reached by a long path having 12 religious stations and are surrounded by tall elegant fir trees.

Cultural design

Local craftsmen meet the needs of communities. They take account of the climate with little reference to formal architectural styles, and have constructed buildings of clay, stone or timber. A variety of distinctive buildings cover the countryside. Where the rock is soft subterranean cave houses have been excavated. Granaries raised on stone stilts to prevent rats climbing up into the grain are a common sight in northern Spain. In fields, shelters for livestock and for storing crops are often seen. Windmills provide power where there is little running water but plentiful wind.

Cathedrals and palaces

Spain has always imported its cultural architecture – Moorish from North Africa, Romanesque and Gothic from France, Renaissance from Italy. Each style, however, has been interpreted in a Spanish way, with contrasts between light and shady areas, façades alternating between the austere and the extravagant, thick walls pierced by few windows to lessen the impact of the sunlight.

DID YOU KNOW?
Industrial archaeology

Windmills

Windmills need the best possible location to utilise their power source. Remains will be found on any piece of high ground near a village, on the coast and on top of cliffs. Near Javea, there are over ten of them on the cliff edge. Today only the ruined towers remain. They were used to grind wheat but now lie unused. Many of the mills date from pre-Moorish times. The wind caught the sails made of canvas which turned wooden shafts and gears attached to large grinding stones.

Watch towers

The authorities built round lookout towers in the sixteenth century on the coast to provide an early warning of pirate raids.

Raids by ships from Africa were quite common. After the final expulsion of the Moors in 1609, the raids became more frequent and the authorities had to take steps to combat them by building towers and by providing a fleet of defensive ships. The coastal towns were, of course, the most vulnerable to attack. In 1636, the pirates, after pillaging Calpe, took nearly all the population back to Algiers. They were released many years later when a ransom had been paid.

Farmhouses

Where there is an extensive farmhouse you will always find a well, an oven and a threshing area known as an *era*. Threshing and crushing of cereals was achieved by means of a metre long tapered stone pulled over the grain on a flat surface. Larger farmhouses had separate accommodation for workers, a small church and a place for children. The animals were held in an open area attached to the house that faced south with a windowless north wall. The key however was a well with water; without it no one survived.

Mozarabic trails

Mozarabic is used to describe narrow stepped trails which cross over mountains from valley to valley. They are true marvels of engineering zigzagging down into the depths of the deepest ravines and up the other side. The trails are characterised by thousands of steps with supporting walls in tricky places. Many have withstood the ravages of time and lack of maintenance. They are best seen in the Val de Laguart south of Valencia. Their use was simply as a communications route from valley to valley over a high mountain.

MORE THAN JUST DALI

Four Spanish grand masters stand out:

◆ Diego de Velázquez, who was a seventeenth-century court portrait painter;

◆ Francisco de Goya depicted Spanish life during one of its most violent periods;

◆ the prolific twentieth-century master Pablo Picasso is recognised as the founder of modern art;

◆ El Greco was born in Crete but lived in Spain, where he painted religious scenes in an individualistic style.

Modern art

The early twentieth-century artists Pablo Picasso and Salvador Dali both belonged to a modern era of art. Born in Malaga, Picasso spent his early years in Barcelona before moving to Paris, where he became famous. It is, however Dali, who has a mysterious reputation. Never far from controversy he embraced a branch of painting called Surrealism, famous for its hallucinatory images. A self-publicist his career included writing and film directing. He died in 1989.

Among many great Spanish collections, the Centro de Reina Sofia in Madrid specialises in modern art and the Prado, also in Madrid, displays historic art. Contemporary artists are accorded great prestige. Their work is seen in town halls, banks and public squares. Towns often have a museum dedicated to a local painter.

QUIXOTE, LORCA, HEMINGWAY AND OTHERS

Miguel de Cervantes was Spain's greatest literary figure. Held captive by the Turks for five years he was almost 60 when he wrote in 1605 the comic masterpiece *Don Quixote*, La Mancha's favourite son. Many iron figures in today's La Mancha are testament to this popular figure and his creator.

> Don Quixote sees only what he believes to be there. His reading of stories about Knights and damsels in distress shape his imagination. Windmills are giants waving their arms in mock defiance. Wine barrels are insolent enemies. He takes them all on, to the amusement of all those who watch and mock. (Cervantes)

Many writers of all nationalities have followed since then. The most popular, emerging at the time of oppression or freedom in the 1960s or 70s are Juan Marse, José Caballero, Antonia Muñoz, and Joan Benet. Foreign writers, such as Dumas, Hemingway, Capek and lately Morris have all described an account of their travels. Hemingway is also renowned for his understanding of bullfighting recorded in his book *Death in the Afternoon*.

Federico García Lorca, born in 1898 near Granada and assassinated by a group of Franco's thugs in 1936, was unquestionably Spain's favourite poet. He achieved fame at the age of 30 with a book of gypsy ballads and based on this success went to America to study. Returning in 1931 he then produced his best works: 1933 – *Blood Wedding*; 1935 – *Yerma*; 1935 – *Death of a Bullfighter* (see Chapter 9); 1936 – *La Casa de Bernarda Alba*.

OPERA, MUSIC AND SEÑOR CHURCH

Spain has produced some of the world's leading opera performers including Victoria de los Angeles, Teresa Berganza, Montserrat Caballe, José Carreras, Placido Domingo and Alfredo Kraus. Regular performances are held in Madrid, Barcelona, Oviedo, Bilbao and other cities. Barcelona has a recognised opera house, the Gran Teatro del Liceu, considered second worldwide only to the La Scala in Milan. An opera house was opened in Seville in 1992.

Spain also stages a wealth of excellent music festivals including a festival of religious music in Cuenca; the international festival of music and dance in Granada which is Spain's most important musical event; the Santander international festival of music, dance and drama; an international music festival in Barcelona; and an autumn festival in Madrid. A wealth of traditional folk music is played on the classical guitar. An International festival of the guitar is held in Córdoba.

Spain's most popular crooner is currently Julio Iglesias, who has sold more records in more languages than any other musical artist in history. Translated, his name is July Church – a clever name for both an international audience and for domestic Roman Catholic fans.

SUMMARY

◆ Spain owes a lot to a rich heritage from the Moors.

◆ Although Spain conquered the world and riches returned to the mother country, vast civilisations were destroyed in the process.

◆ Franco's legacy was a cruel and bloody civil war followed by a vindictive peace.

◆ The mountains in the north, the wetlands in the southeast and the volcanic landscapes of the Canaries are some of nature's stunning attractions.

◆ Spain's farming is diverse. Traditional almond, orange and olive groves contrast with the vast rolling wheat fields and 'market gardening' under protective cover. Don't forget the unusual cork tree.

◆ The *plaza mayor* and the *ermita* are both landmarks in towns and villages throughout Spain.

◆ Spain's industrial heritage can be seen in the country – windmills, watch towers, trails and farmhouses.

◆ Picasso and Dali are among the better-known Spanish painters. Picasso was born in Spain but came to fame in France. Dali represents Surrealism.

◆ *Don Quixote* by Cervantes, Lorca's verse and *Death in the Afternoon* by Hemingway are only some literary works worthy of mention.

$$\left(\, 3 \,\right)$$

Preparing to Go

THE DOCUMENTS REQUIRED

The EU allows free movement in its member states for all its citizens, provided they have a National Identity Card or a passport. The UK is one of the few countries in Europe that does not issue an ID card, possibly due to the high cost of introduction and domestic political pressures. This may change as European integration takes place. Until ID cards are introduced in the UK a current valid passport is required for its citizens to enter Spain and for internal identification purposes thereafter.

A person on a short-term stay from within or outside the EU can enter Spain with as little as:

- a passport;
- Form E111 for temporary reciprocal medical cover;
- a Driving Licence;
- some euros;
- a credit card – since the introduction of the euro virtually all *bureaux de change* have disappeared but ATMs (cash dispenser machines) take all international debit cards.

EU immigration law is simple but things do get slightly more complicated if you are a non-EU resident or an EU resident entering the country for a long stay.

Visitors to Spain for up to 90 days from all countries only need a passport.

Citizens of non-EU countries require a visa from the Spanish Consulate before coming to Spain to work, study or live. The visa is stamped in the passport. Documentary evidence to obtain a visa is stringent depending on the reason for entry. Proof of financial resources, medical health cover and no criminal record are the basic requirements. An employment contract or proof of admission to a Spanish educational establishment, or letter from a family if an au pair are all additional requirements. A non-EU national also requires a work permit, secured by a prospective employer from the *Delagación Provincial de Ministerio de Trabajo.*

All EU residents when taking up a new life in Spain, for work or retirement, must apply for a *número de identificacion de extranjero* (NIE for short or NIF for the Spanish equivalent) and *residencia* if intending to spend more than 182 days per calendar year in the country. Details of this are contained in Chapter 12. A work permit is not required.

When moving to Spain permanently, or for a lengthy stay, it is wise to take with you, as appropriate:

- birth and marriage certificates;
- facilities to open a new bank account, if setting up a business;

◆ CV, preferably in Spanish of course, if seeking employment;

◆ vehicle documents, if temporarily driving a car registered outside Spain.

Bureaucracy is always an issue, but Spain does have a problem with illegal Moroccan immigrants and the tolerant authorities giving periodic amnesties. In certain areas these immigrants are responsible for 80% of the petty crime. Many Northern Europeans live permanently in Spain without an NIE or *residencia* and without paying taxes – they are illegal immigrants too but their passports protect them from full legal penalties.

DID YOU KNOW?
20th and 21st century Moors

There has always been a tolerant attitude between the people of Spain and Morocco. This, however, has not always been the case with governments. Between the World Wars, poison gas was used in colonial wars despite the Versailles Treaty ban on the use of chemical weapons. Probably the least known of these chemical offensives was waged by Spain against the Moroccans in the Rif War of 1919–27.

Three years after the First World War, Spain reached a secret agreement with a German gas producer to supply chemicals and technicians to make the gas. Evading Allied controls, these were transported to Spain and Morocco, and factories were converted in both countries to produce mustard gas. Between 1921 and 1927, vast quantities of the gas were dropped on civilian targets in northern Morocco.

The deadly effects of mustard gas were well known to the European powers from its use in the First World War. Mustard gas survivors are prone to die of cancer, and prima facie evidence indicates that the cancer produced by the gas can be passed on genetically. Figures suggest the rate of childhood cancer is much higher in those areas bombed with mustard gas by the Spanish than elsewhere in Morocco.

Today the people of Spain are accustomed to seeing Moroccan families returning to their homeland. They work in the EU and are returning home for a holiday heading to the ferry port of Algeciras. A few weeks later they will make the return journey, minus the large bulbous roof rack of goods left with the gold braided customs officials at Tangier. They will tell their brothers in the souks of the wealth in Germany, the liberal ways of France, the warmth of Spain. They have a legal job and the necessary papers, but their brothers don't.

Consequently there is another type of immigrant to the EU and particularly Spain – an illegal immigrant, one who comes in the hope of securing a job and a brighter future. How do they get to Spain? They come in small open boats, normally used for inshore fishing and powered by an outboard engine. Many die, as the Straits of Gibraltar are a dangerous place with strong currents, high winds and inclement weather. They may also be put over the side to swim to a beach.

Thousands of Moroccans do make it to the interior of Spain. Those who are not picked up by the police face an uncertain future with no documents and confined to low paid jobs. Those that are picked up are difficult to expel because they refuse to say where they come from.

WHAT CLOTHING TO TAKE

This is best addressed by answering a few questions.

- How long am I staying?
- What is the time of year on arrival?
- How many seasons will I be there?
- Am I affected by heat or cold?
- Should I buy some clothes in Spain?

The Spanish dress well in all walks of life. The choice of shoes and clothing is wide. Dress and appearance is important if doing business with Spanish counterparts. It pays to make a little of effort. Men usually wear ties, but are not necessarily restricted to a suit, as often a smart jacket will suffice. Ladies tend to wear elegant clothing, often with a jacket.

In summer months it can be unbearably hot, so white cotton clothing to deflect the sun, cool footwear and a hat, together with lots of T-shirts and shorts for leisure wear, are all that is required. In the evening a lightweight sweater may be necessary.

In the autumn it is still very warm, so summer clothing will suffice, with additionally a jumper or jacket in the evening. By the sea, or in the mountains, it can be cool.

It is possible to sunbathe in sheltered spots in the winter but January, February and even March can all be wet, cold and miserable. It is possible to get snow too! Many people are unprepared without warm clothing, water-proofs and suitable footwear.

Spring brings the emerging warm sunshine. Clothing, which suited autumn conditions, will again be adequate. As the weeks progress the layers peel off.

When new residents from Northern Europe first come to Spain they find the summers very hot. They sweat profusely and often feel tired and lethargic. In winter they are comfortable but surprised to see Spaniards wrapped up heavily with coats and scarves.

After two years they acclimatise. The shorts worn in autumn and spring are replaced with long trousers. Summer is comfortable. Winter is cold. If they go back to Germany, Scandinavia or the UK, they freeze. The climate has not changed, but the individual has.

TAKING YOUR PETS

There is absolutely no reason why a pet cannot be taken to Spain, or for that matter travel through an inter-mediate country such as France. The United Kingdom has recently relaxed its views on quarantine regulations bringing its approach in line with other European countries. It may be necessary to travel to and from Spain frequently or unexpectedly, in which case any pet should have the necessary vaccinations, health checks and accompanying paperwork.

Spain has the normal catteries and kennels. It has many fully qualified veterinary surgeons. Towns and cities have codes of behaviour for dogs which result in them being banned from beaches and other public places.

There is another side to keeping a pet in Spain. Dogs are usually working animals, or are often tied up all day, left to roam or even simply abandoned. Cats multiply and roam wild. Rabbits are for consumption. The Spanish are not a nation of animal lovers. There are dog refuge organisations in most costal towns, invariably run by resident Britons or Germans who often witness many barbaric acts committed upon these defenceless animals.

Sport and cruelty are sometimes indistinguishable. In addition to dog cruelty any wild bird is a prime target. Birds are indiscriminately shot for food and netted, using water as bait or by employing birdlime made of boiled wine. The more colourful specimens are trapped, using a captive bird as a lure, then sold in small cages as song birds to end their days on a town balcony.

LEARNING THE LANGUAGE

Spanish business people can generally speak English and German in addition to their native tongue. Waiters and shop assistants too can often manage a few English words. Builders, repairmen, installation engineers, petrol attendants, postmen, policemen and hospital staff generally speak only Spanish.

It is just about possible to live in Spain without speaking Spanish. Interpreters or friends can be used as an aid to discussion. The use of body language, pointing, nodding and shrugging can also assist. Enhancement of communication with a few key words such as *si*, *una*, *por favor*, *gracias* (not necessarily in that order) is a step in the right direction. But the non-linguist needs one other major phrase: '*¿Hable Inglés, por favor?*' (Can you speak English please?).

There can be no substitute for learning the basics of the Spanish language. After all, it is their country we are choosing to visit or live in. We can surely be polite and respectful by learning a few words. If you are a student, or wish to work in a professional occupation, learning the language is a necessity.

How do you learn the language? Home study courses by book and audiotapes are heavily advertised. These courses are an intensive learning medium. Timing is best suited to the individual.

Many intensive language schools operate in Spain with prospectuses aimed at a variety of levels in many European languages. Contact the British Council in Madrid. They are big in Spain, covering language, teaching and cultural exchange.

One of the best learning methods before leaving home is an old fashioned adult evening class at a local school or college. A bit of fun and a common purpose together with some effort for 20–25 evenings will get the average person to a decent basic linguistic standard.

Remember the Spanish language is *Castellano*. A good example of the complexities of a regional dialect and pronunciation is given below:

◆ Jalon – the name of a town spelt in *Castellano* and written on national maps;

- Xalon – the same town spelt in the *Valenciano* dialect seen on signposts;

- Halon – how to pronounce it in any dialect.

LETTING THE HOUSE BACK HOME

Some people, having purchased a Spanish home with the intention of living here permanently, are reluctant to sell their old home. Retaining a base back home gives a bolthole in the event of a change in circumstance.

It makes sense to put the letting of a property in the hands of experts. The Association of Residential Agents, formed in 1981, regulates letting agents and seeks to promote the provision of high standards of service to both landlords and tenants. Membership is restricted to those letting agents who can demonstrate good financial practices and have a good working knowledge of all the legal issues involved.

If the owner is classed as an overseas resident for tax purposes, the letting company is responsible for deducting income tax at base rate on the rental income, unless the Inland Revenue provides a tax exemption certificate.

A letting company will charge around 15% of the rental income for a full service together with charges for introducing tenants and drawing up agreements. Taxation and letting charges can therefore reduce gross letting income by 30 to 40%.

MOVING YOUR FURNITURE

Spanish furniture is attractive, distinctive and ornate, but is not to everyone's taste. Moving comfortable furniture from home, bits and pieces that one has grown accustomed to, is often preferred.

European removal companies are sound professional organisations belonging to the International Federation of Furniture Removers. They have well-established operational and administrative procedures. Packing and paperwork is left to them. While it is obvious that more than one competitive quote is necessary, the cheapest company should be one which offers a shared service with depots close to both the old home and the new Spanish home. The cost of moving an average home, including insurance, calculated according to the number of cubic metres required is at present around €3,500 to €5,000. Cost reduction is best achieved by flexibility in pick-up and delivery dates. Transit time is approximately two weeks.

It is wise to leave TV sets at home as the Spanish sound system and the receiving frequency differ from other European countries. Washing machines work successfully but the plumbing of a Spanish home does not allow for a hot water fill. Computers, vacuum cleaners and other domestic items all operate successfully on Spanish voltages but all electrical appliances will require an adaptor from a three to a two-pin plug.

For furniture transported by road, the EU's relaxation on border controls means that arrival in Spain via another EU country should not be subject to any formal customs procedures. For effects arriving by sea or air, ensure all the relevant documentation is to hand.

As an alternative to moving furniture from home, all items can be purchased in Spain. Furniture packages to equip an entire home are readily available. They come in different sizes, style and quality. The range can cover a simple two-bedroom holiday home, to a large expensive package in a distinctive, colourful, Spanish style for a permanent home.

ORGANISING YOUR TRAVEL

Flights

There are daily scheduled flights to Spain by recognised major national carriers and the Spanish carrier Iberia. Standard fares are charged.

However, the cheapest and most frequently used method of air travel is a last-minute booking on a charter flight or low-cost carrier currently at around €55 one-way. Tickets are best obtained from a flight-only shop, direct from a low-cost carrier, or through the many Internet sites devoted to low cost travel.

Alicante, Málaga, Majorca and Tenerife are the most frequently used Spanish airports. Within Spain a daily shuttle service operates between Madrid and its regional capitals.

Data from the Association of European Airlines shows that 24% of European flights were delayed by more than 15 minutes. Madrid is the worst with 36% of departures delayed for on average 43 minutes and Gatwick is one of the best with only 19% of flights delayed.

Ferry

The following international ferries operate:

- Plymouth or Portsmouth to Santander – twice weekly;
- Portsmouth to Bilbao – twice weekly;
- Algeciras to Tangier or Ceuta – several sailings per day;
- Gibraltar to Tangier – daily;
- Málaga or Almeria to Melilla – daily.

Within Spain the following domestic services operate:

- Cádiz to the Canaries – daily;
- Barcelona, Valencia or Denia to the Balearics – daily;
- Inter-Island ferries operating within the Canaries and the Balearics.

Car hire

It makes sense to pre-book car hire at the same time as booking air or ferry tickets. It avoids waiting on arrival, as the car should be ready. All the international car hire companies operate in Spain together with many Spanish national and regional operators. It is a fiercely competitive market. *Coche de alquilar* (car hire) can also be booked at airports or in large towns.

E-commerce

Travel is the fastest growing area of e-commerce. The web and travel go very well together. It is a service. There is nothing to deliver other than the confirmation of a booking. Information can be updated very quickly online, making it perfect for accessing the latest deals. Booking flights, ferries or arranging car rental are achieved by a few mouse clicks.

PREPARING FOR CULTURE SHOCK

Preparing to go to Spain is not just about a physical change. A few weeks after landing in a new country the shock of a different culture, changes in attitude and frequent frustration can have an adverse effect on one's well-being. Isolation, feeling powerless and finding fault with everyone are classic symptoms. The blow can be cushioned if an understanding has been reached before-hand about Spanish ways and understanding the symptoms can also help to assimilate the change.

The first stage is a honeymoon period, which everyone experiences. It can be followed by a period of feeling inadequate, lonely, withdrawn and wanting to go back home. But by being positive and becoming more assertive, you soon find you can deal with situations and start to feel more relaxed. The final stage is feeling at home, embracing the new culture.

SUMMARY

- ◆ The documents required to enter Spain can range from a simple passport or ID card for EU citizens on holiday, or complex visa requirements for non-EU residents on a long-term stay.

- ◆ Future residents of Spain require an NIE and a *residencia*.

- ◆ Spain has a problem with illegal immigrants from North Africa.

- Clothing depends on the season, the length of stay and how quickly you acclimatise.

- By all means take your pet but remember Spain is not renowned for its love of animals.

- It is better to learn the basics of the Spanish language. It makes day-to-day communication easier.

- Letting out your property back home is best achieved through a professionally recognised agent.

- Many furniture removal companies have depots in Spain.

- Travel is best achieved through buying tickets from flight-only shops, low-cost airlines or through the ever increasing numbers of Internet booking services.

- Prepare for the culture shock.

4

Getting the Facts on Retirement

No one can offer a blueprint for perfect retirement. Life experience, knowledge, preferences, capabilities and knowing what is wanted from retirement are some factors to be considered. It is a period of change, a transition from one stage of life to another. At retirement people are faced with changes in responsibility, relationships, ways to use time, challenges to personal philosophy and changes in financial position. The major changes can be summarised in terms of income, health and lifestyle.

PLANNING YOUR INCOME

Sources of income at retirement are usually:

- state retirement pension;
- company and personal pensions;
- investments and savings.

State retirement pension

The UK state retirement pension is made up of the following components:

- basic pension;
- graduated pension;
- additional pension;

- ◆ SERPS – state earnings related pension;
- ◆ any extra pension for dependents.

The size of pension depends on the contributions made to the National Insurance scheme during a person's working life in the UK and how many of those years were qualifying years. Retirement pensions are paid to beneficiaries at the rate prevailing in the UK if resident in Spain, although this is not the case with all countries.

The European picture is shown in Figure 2.

Country	Year 2000	Year 2002
United Kingdom	5.1%	4.6%
Belgium	9.3%	12.1%
Germany	10.5%	12.7%
Spain	9.4%	13.2%
France	12.1%	15.7%
Ireland	7.6%	4.6%
Italy	14.2%	16.1%
Holland	7.9%	12.8%
Austria	14.5%	18.3%
Portugal	9.4%	14.7%
Finland	11.3%	15.9%
Sweden	9.0%	11.6%

Figure 2. European pension costs (*source: EU*)

The figures demonstrate the percentage gross domestic product that countries will have to spend to maintain state pension payments. Only in the United Kingdom and Ireland will demands on the taxpayer fall due to a strong private pensions industry. Other countries rely on generous state-funded schemes now under heavy pressure.

Company and personal pensions

The principal of pensions is straightforward but constant changes in the law have allowed a greater number of options. In an occupational pension, one or more parties have invested money over a number of years. The pension is paid out, usually with an inflation element, according to the rules of the scheme as set by the trustees based on final salary and the number of years in the scheme.

Annuities, however, are a bit more complicated. An annuity is a regular income bought with a lump sum. In the last ten years annuity rates have fallen by 40%. They are based on the average life expectancy and the long-term yields of government bonds. Life expectancy has increased while yields have fallen, which is doubly bad news for annuities.

There are three types of annuity. Level annuities are paid at the same amount each year but the purchasing power is eroded by inflation. Escalating annuities ratchet up by a set percentage each year but the bigger the escalation the lower the income to start with. Lastly, index-linked annuities can follow routes such as the Retail Price Index.

Some pensions are best left alone, some better converted to annuities. A flexible pension taken out in the later years of life according to one's need is excellent. A choice of pension is a major decision. Once done, that is it, for the rest of your life.

One final thought: 'People need to appreciate that they cannot work from 25 to 55 then live the life of O'Riley to 95.' So stated the chairman of the National Association of Pension Funds. He may be right, or he may be wrong. Appendix 4 has the headings for a do-it-yourself ready-reckoner to calculate income before and after retirement.

Investments and savings

Investments are more flexible although each one should be entered into with a long-term strategy. Investments are about risk, with risk being relative to each person. Reward follows risk – it is the law of economics.

Risk can be categorised, ranging from inflation risk to gambling risk, but most investments focus on geographical, sectional and equity risk. Geographical risk involves a part of the world such as the UK, Europe or the USA. Sectional risk involves investing in a sector such as technology, retail or food. Equity risk relates to the investment type such as bonds, shares or unit trusts.

At the bottom of the risk ladder are building societies, corporate bonds and government stocks. Going up the risk ladder are tracker funds that mirror the FTSE 100 and shares in companies. Near the top are overseas investments or themed investments such as technology stocks. At the top are volatile futures dealings.

DID YOU KNOW?
Investing offshore

The term 'offshore' has no legal definition. Investing offshore does not necessarily mean placing capital with a bank or investment company based on an island. The reference to offshore infers that private investors are making financial transactions in a jurisdiction different from their normal residence for tax purposes. It is thought that half of the world's capital is invested within international offshore financial centres, also known as tax havens.

The best-known offshore centres are the Isle of Man, Jersey, Guernsey and Gibraltar. Land based popular offshore centres are Luxembourg, Switzerland and Liechtenstein. The more distant well-known offshore tax havens are Bermuda, the Bahamas, and the British Virgin Islands. There are more than 50 well-established international tax havens.

Why invest offshore? The most common reason for private investors to place capital offshore is to reduce tax. Banks and financial institutions invariably pay less tax in respect of subsidiaries based in offshore locations. For example, identical insurance investment funds based in London and the Isle of Man would not perform the same. This is because UK-based companies deduct tax at source on income and make allowances for capital gains tax on unrealised gains. The same fund located offshore would suffer little or no tax

One of the more secure investments is an offshore with-profits investment bond, this being a tax-efficient single-life insurance policy, offered by a number of reputable investment companies with offices in Luxembourg, the Isle of Man or Guernsey. There is a choice of investment and the opportunity for regular withdrawals. The key is that the investment stays in the offshore geographical location, the gains not being affected by the place of residence. Responsibility for the declaration of withdrawals rests with the investor.

A word of warning! European law is changing. Offshore banks are now obliged to disclose any interest gained in bank accounts to the tax authorities in the country where the account holder resides. or implement a withholding tax. Some people speculate that further legislation may occur limiting the benefits of offshore investments.

Inheritance Trusts

Protection from taxation and inheritance legalisation can be achieved by setting up an offshore trust fund, which initially sounds expensive and complex but in practice can be achieved simply by organisations specialising in this type of work. Protection of a property from inheritance tax is not possible under a trust.

Getting professional advice

Financial advisers may be independent and able to choose from any company's services. They may be tied agents who only offer the range of products from the investment house that employs them. Insurance companies too have their representatives, but they may also employ others on a freelance basis to represent their products.

In most European countries, these agents will be members of a recognised professional organisation, be independent and subject to legal scrutiny. Before choosing an adviser, do they know about Spain? Do they know about Spanish taxation, offshore investments and Spanish inheritance tax? If not then they are not ideal. It is a waste of time undertaking financial planning embracing the laws of another country when it is the laws of Spain that have to be considered.

Spanish financial advisers are not so well regulated as those in other countries. They even sell their 'own label' products. It does not mean they are bad. It simply means that one has to be more cautious when dealing with money matters in Spain. When dealing with investments remember the quickest way to double your money is to fold it in half, put it back in your pocket and not to be seduced by newspaper advertisements offering exceptionally high returns.

KEEPING HEALTHY

Physical health

An individual is responsible for his or her own health and the need to maintain it. Fitness is how efficiently the heart works, how strong the muscles are and how easy it is to bend and stretch.

- Can you walk uphill or run for a bus without getting out of breath?

- Can you walk up two flights of stairs or carry a load of shopping home without getting tired?

- Can you bend down to weed the garden or reach up to clean the windows without difficulty?

- Is your body mass index in the range 20–25? For the uninitiated the index is calculated by dividing body weight in kilograms by height in metres squared.

It's never too late to start getting more exercise. Get moving, move a little more, build up gradually, and keep it going. Exercise does not have to be physical jerks or jogging in a tracksuit. Do something enjoyable. Walking and swimming are very good non-impact exercises.

There's no shortage of advice about what to eat and what not to eat. The guidelines are clear. Cut down on fat, sugar and salt. Eat lean meat, fish and fibre with plenty of fresh fruit and vegetables. But knowing it is one thing, doing it is another as we learn our eating habits very early in life.

Mental health

To keep happy we probably need to be with other people at least some of the time, to be involved in warm and friendly relationships, to have someone to talk to and to play a part in what's going on inside the family and the community. As we get older it becomes more important to think about maintaining and strengthening friendships, keeping in touch with people we like and making opportunities to meet new friends.

A feeling of stress and strain can spoil happiness. Losing a close friend or relative, losing a job, or changing familiar surroundings can make people ill. We cannot avoid stress. What we can do is be aware of how we react to it, notice our own warning signals, and take some positive action to keep it in check.

It is important in retirement to maintain a sense of purpose. Motivation for working – whatever that may have been – at least gave a sense of purpose. Transferring energies towards enjoyable activities, or new commitments, is a way of maintaining that sense of purpose.

A NEW LIFESTYLE

Men and women follow different life and career patterns. A traditional picture shows a man going out to work and a woman, perhaps after caring for children, going back to work but still having the role of looking after children and relatives. The retirement of one partner needs to be thought about in terms of how their relationship will be affected by this change. Each person's expectations of retirement may be different.

Whether the choice is early retirement, voluntary redundancy or retirement at the normal age, or unexpectedly being in these situations, there are a number of issues to explore. Any change in personal circumstances presents an opportunity to positively reassess lifestyle. To stagnate or move forward is a choice.

THE FREQUENCY OF MOVING HOUSE

In affluent countries most people passing from working to retirement find their income, housing needs and physical capabilities all reduce. These changes alter housing requirements and preferences. Men who attain 85 years of age on average move 1.06 times after their 55th birthday, and women 1.14 times. While most are local moves, a minority are long-distance changes.

Since the 1920s, retirement migrations have become commonplace and have passed through several phases. During the 1930s and 1950s, railway-influenced holiday destinations guided retirement moves from the UK's large cities to numerous resorts in Devon, Dorset, Somerset, Sussex, Kent, Essex, Lancashire, Yorkshire and North Wales. From the 1960s, the destinations dispersed to unspoilt market towns and well-serviced villages, as in Dorset, the Cotswolds, and Central Wales, and most recently to Lincolnshire and Yorkshire. In the 1990s the choice was to resort and rural settings in France, Spain and other southern European countries (see Figure 3).

Rank	Country	Number	% change 1988 to 1999	% share
1	Australia	198,000	59	24
2	Canada	134,000	60	17
3	USA	112,000	42	14
4	Ireland	87,000	67	11
5	Spain	39,000	**105**	5
6	South Africa	33,000	23	4
7	New Zealand	32,000	9	4
8	Italy	28,000	41	4
9	Germany	25,000	89	3
10	Jamaica	24,000	77	3
11	France	16,000	**158**	2
12	Others	66,000	N/A	9

Figure 3. Spain – in the top two for increase in overseas retirement

Some reasons for staying put

If you enjoy your home, it fits your needs and you can afford it, then why move? If you stay in a place where you have friends, neighbours, children living close by and you know your way around, then why move? If the facilities and services are good, then why move? After all, moving is a lot of trouble and expense.

Some reasons for moving

If your house is too big, too expensive or the capital tied up in it could provide income if invested, then consider moving. If the area is deteriorating or the community does not offer social, cultural or physical activities and lacks services, then consider moving. If your health would benefit from warm sunshine, then move. If your children and friends have moved away, then why stay?

Who buys a home abroad?

A wide range of people buy a home in the sun, particularly if it is near an airport, faces the sea or a golf course and the area has plenty of facilities. If it is a permanent retirement home then the average profile is of a couple, mid fifties and upwards, whose children have flown the nest. At least one partner will be an extrovert capable of dealing with the upheaval and change, so together they can look forward to their golden years with some enthusiasm. The responsibilities of unpaid carer of children, grandchildren or looking after elderly parents are issues that have been dealt with.

Moving abroad is a challenge, an adventure, a new culture and a different lifestyle. As life expectancy increases moving abroad is now commonplace. In the last 20 years the number of retirees living abroad has doubled. However, the number of people from the UK retiring to Spain has doubled in ten years.

Most people who retire abroad are fully fit, active and in possession of all their faculties. Unfortunately as age increases health may fail and we become partly dependent or totally dependent on partners, friends and special housing or welfare facilities. Care for the elderly in Spain falls upon the family with sheltered housing rare.

THE RESULTS OF THE INTERNATIONAL PASSENGER SURVEY

The UK International Passenger Survey samples between

0.1% and 0.5% of the passengers that enter or leave through seaports, airports and the Channel Tunnel It establishes the age, sex and citizenship of the traveller, and asks both emigrants and immigrants whether they are moving for work or study. Unfortunately, neither a retirement move nor joining a family is distinguished as a reason.

Since 1980 an average of 11,300 men and 6,600 women in late working age (45–59 years for women, and 45–64 years for men) have emigrated from the UK each year. In this age group the main categories are:

♦ UK citizens moving to another country for work;

♦ non-UK citizens returning to their countries of origin or moving elsewhere;

♦ UK citizens retiring early abroad.

There have been sharp annual fluctuations in the total number of emigrants. The total rose during the mid-1980s to 23,000 but in 1988 the housing market boom in southern England collapsed and the number of emigrants decreased. There was another emigration peak in 1993. In the following three years the total oscillated around 17,000 and in 1999 it rose sharply to 24,500.

Since 1980 the annual average number of departures from the UK of people of state pensionable age has been 2,320 men and 4,660 women. The numbers have a high female-to-male ratio, the principal explanation being that many of the emigrants are widowed, divorced or single women leaving to live with or near relatives and friends who settled earlier abroad.

STATISTICS FROM NEWCASTLE

The Pensions and Overseas Benefits Directorate in the UK, based at Newcastle, record a second source of information on the number of people living abroad. Beneficiaries fall into three categories: those receiving state pensions, widows' benefits and 'unclassified'.

It is well known that the British population in various Mediterranean locations is not clearly defined between tourists, seasonal residents, temporary residents and permanent residents. It is difficult for these categories to correspond tidily with legal and administrative headings as 'resident foreigner', 'taxpayer' or 'local elector'. Further confusion arises as many people retain a property and bank account in the UK, finding it convenient to maintain a base back home. However, there have been recent technological and commercial changes in retail banking which, with changing tax regimes, has led to a rising proportion of people requesting that their state pension payments are paid to a bank in their adopted country.

There has been a substantial increase in the number of overseas state pensioners (see Figure 4). Starting at a quarter of a million in 1981 they have now more than doubled at an annual growth rate of 8.95%. Growth was high at 10% during 1988–89 at the end of the 'Lawson boom' when the exceptional inflation in UK house prices fuelled a high rate of overseas property purchases. During the 1990s growth moderated to 3.5% per annum.

Date	UK state pensioners based overseas	% annual growth rate
1981	252	N/A
1986	372	8.1
1991	594	9.8
1996	763	5.1
1999	847	3.5
1981 to 1999	N/A	6.9

Figure 4. The growth in numbers of UK pensioners overseas

The average age of overseas pensioners is younger than that of the similar home population. This differential is more pronounced among women. Younger male overseas pensioners (aged 65–74 years) outnumbered the older (75+ years) by 60%, compared with 46% in the 1999 home population. Among women, the younger outnumbered the older by 48%.

Turning now to male/female statistics – the ratio of women to men resident abroad was 1.26, whereas according to the 1999 mid-year estimates, the ratio in the UK resident population was 1.42

British pensioners in 1999 received their state benefits in more than 200 countries. Of the 814,000 nearly a quarter were in Australia and a substantial number in the USA, the Irish Republic and Canada. Surprisingly these four countries account for nearly two-thirds of the total. But the countries with high growth rates are southern European countries with sunbelt retirement locations such as Spain, France, Italy and European countries that are near neighbours of the UK who have strong economic, social and working links. When considering only countries with at least 10,000 British pensioners, the highest rates of increase during 1994 to 1999 were in Italy, Spain, France and the USA.

SEEKING MORE THAN PLEASANT AMENITIES

Contrary to the widespread view, British and other over-seas-retired populations are not predominantly composed of those who work and live in their own countries until their late fifties or sixties and then undertake a pleasant and agreeable move to a sunny location on the Spanish Costas. The pathway to overseas retirement is much more complex than simply a move to sun-drenched resorts.

Widespread multinational processes and specific historical factors are involved. The growth rate in each destination country is subject to the vagaries of political events, the local economy and, in some cases, the legacies of a military and imperial past.

Other people return to the 'old country', a sequel to the extensive and increasingly global labour migrations that began in the 1950s. A large number of British pensioners are evident in the Republic of Ireland.

Lastly, the substantial number of UK pensioners in Germany and the high growth rates in several close European countries reflect the British population's changing overseas employment and family connections through higher education, civic exchanges, skilled labour demand, armed forces and temporary work placements. When a country has both numerous opportunities for retirees to join their family and an attractive environment, then migrations are obviously high, as in, for example, the Mediterranean countries.

While the international redistribution of older people may be small in comparison to the number of economic migrants and refugees, there is huge potential for growth as demographic ageing, the falling cost of international air travel and rising affluence among many people will combine to increase the number of returning, family-joining and amenity-seeking migrants.

SUMMARY

◆ Retirement is a transition from one stage of life to another.

◆ Income, health and lifestyle are major change factors.

◆ A good financial adviser, one with knowledge of Spanish legislation, is necessary.

◆ Offshore investments are 'better' than conventional investments.

◆ Keep healthy – prepare for the enjoyment of a new lifestyle.

◆ About 1% of the population move house after reaching age 55.

◆ Moving back to the 'old country' is a popular retirement choice.

- Moving abroad is increasing – it is an adventure and a challenge.

- Italy, Spain, France and the USA have the highest growth rates of UK state pensioners.

- Not all moves are simply to high amenity areas close to the Mediterranean. Many people join a family or go to where work has previously been undertaken.

Working in Spain

LANGUAGE – THE MAIN REQUIREMENT

The most important requirement for anyone seeking employment is the ability to speak good Spanish. The dominance of regional languages and dialects causes problems for foreigners and Spaniards from other parts of Spain. But if seeking professional employment, learning the language, *Castillano* or a regional variation, is the only option.

Speaking only English restricts job opportunities to servicing the English speaking community. English may be the language of international business but in dealing with Spanish people, or fitting into a multilingual work environment, the ability to converse in Spanish is essential.

EQUAL OPPORTUNITY

Members of EU countries will be treated equally with Spanish nationals. Despite no employment restrictions and a theoretical policy that any EU national can take up work wherever they wish, Spanish applicants for any job may be viewed more favourably.

A multinational company

Working in Spain for a UK company or for one whose name is recognisable worldwide can offer security.

However, a team of Spanish nationals runs most of the Spanish branches of multinational companies and most of the work is conducted in their language. There is a need to fit in.

Spanish companies

They may have a bias towards their own nationals when offering work. However, a native English speaker may be considered an asset but if possessing little knowledge of Spanish the choice of job will remain limited.

British entertainers working on short-term contracts often report a lack of motivation and a certain authoritarian style while working for Spanish employers. It is of course supply and demand in the labour market that counts but other people too question the less than democratic skills and employment practices. 'Unquestionably sharp' is a phrase adequately describing the employment style of some Spanish companies.

Take care

It can be easy to get carried away by the seemingly casual lifestyle, the laid-back approach and amicable business methods, but remember it is profit and customer service that counts. Don't assume that working for an English-speaking northern European gives added security. Spain is full of ex-pats who for one reason or another have decided to make a living through running a bar or a shop, or property dealing. Often the business is very fragile.

CASUAL, SEASONAL, PART-TIME OR FULL-TIME WORK

The type of employment sought will depend on the following factors:

- how long you intend to stay there;
- where you intend to stay;
- your qualifications, skills and experience;
- family support and outgoings.

Casual or seasonal

This type of work is ideal for anyone who has not firmed up a long-term life plan or seeking a few euros while enjoying a life in the sun. It is not too easy to come by, usually involves lots of asking around, and may need a personal recommendation. Work of this nature is more likely to be found in tourist regions where there is a seasonal demand for labour. The best example of this is a courier or rep's job with a major holiday company.

Further examples are:

- agencies for villa servicing and cleaning
- auxiliary nursing
- construction work
- courier or driving jobs
- fruit picking
- gardening
- ice cream salesperson
- promotional work
- restaurants and hotels for waiting or kitchen work
- shop assistant.

Part-time

For someone staying long term and needing a little extra income, some help may be found from the few job agencies, but asking around is essential. Without a command of the language you again are restricted to the holiday regions. Examples of part-time work are:

◆ office work
◆ supermarkets
◆ teaching English
◆ working in a multilingual estate agent's office.

Full-time

Seeking a permanent, professional position? The procedure is exactly the same as back home. Employment agencies, direct contact with companies, word of mouth and personal contact are all necessary. A good CV in English and Spanish, to sell your skills, is helpful. Working full time involves a different working day, correct business etiquette, payment of social security and income tax.

People who are fluent in Spanish and English can find work in the major cities as translators and interpreters where the task involves business correspondence or assisting northern Europeans with some Spanish paperwork, or even at police stations on busy market days where petty theft is common and an interpreter is necessary.

TEACHING

Staying long term in Spain? Then the chances of finding teaching work are considerably better than any other profession. Obviously it depends very much on the qualifications and experience offered.

Teaching English is big business. The Spanish wish to have a second language. For commercial reasons it has to be English. There is a constant demand for teachers. People with a 'Teaching English as a Foreign Language' qualification or 'English as a Second Language' certificate can sometimes find a job quite easily. Where demand outstrips supply in big cities a graduate native English speaker can get a job without other qualifications.

Some of the opportunities are:

◆ Private language schools in Spain offering English classes for both adults and children.

◆ English teachers and teachers employed in language schools can supplement their income by giving private lessons.

◆ The British Council in Madrid recruits English language teachers and supervisory staff for two-year placements in its language centres in Barcelona, Bilbao, Granada, Las Palmas, Madrid, Oviedo, Palma de Mallorca, Segovia, Seville and Valencia. Their website is worth a visit (see Appendix 11).

◆ Being a Language Assistant enables students from Britain and more than 30 other countries to spend a year working in a school or college in Spain assisting language teachers.

YOUR CONTRACT OF EMPLOYMENT

Employment conditions
Employment conditions vary throughout Europe. The main areas of international comparison lie in salary level, fringe benefits and job security. In general Spanish employees are

near the bottom of the European earnings league. However, good fringe benefits with lots of holidays and protection under dismissal legislation are plus factors.

Spain has lost more production days due to strikes in the last ten years than any country in the EU. The government can enforce an imposed settlement if a strike impairs public services or disrupts important sectors of the economy. However, employees are guaranteed the right to strike under law and cannot be dismissed for striking.

The contract

Employees in Spain, like other parts of Europe, have an employment contract (*contrato de trabajo*), stating details such as job title, position, salary, working hours, fringe benefits and the terms of employment.

There are three types of employment contract.

◆ an indefinite term contract;

◆ a short-term contract for a specified period and reason;

◆ a contract for casual or seasonal work, which carries few legal rights.

Salary

A salary is stated in the employment contract together with any salary reviews, planned increases and cost of living reviews. Salaries can be paid weekly, fortnightly or monthly, cash or into a bank account. A pay slip itemising salary and deductions is issued.

Extra months' salary and bonuses

Most employers in Spain pay their employees two extra months' salary – one paid in July before the annual summer holiday and the other in December – which are intended to ensure that employees have extra money for their summer and Christmas holidays. Some companies pay as many as 15 or 16 months' salary, although this is exceptional and may be performance linked.

Working hours

The standard working week in Spain is 40 hours and the average with overtime around 42 hours. The normal working day is from 9.30 am to 13.30 pm and from 16.30 pm until 19.30 pm or 20.30 pm, although from June and September the working day may be continuous from 7.00 am to 15.00 pm.with a short break for lunch. In line with their European counterparts many companies operate from 8.30 am or 9.00 am to 17.30 pm or 18.00 pm. There are no scheduled coffee breaks but it's common for office workers in a town or city to pop out for breakfast or a cup of coffee, twice a day during business hours.

Social security

All employees, including foreign employees and the self-employed, must contribute to the Spanish social security system (*seguridad social*). Social security for employees covers health care (including sickness and maternity leave), injuries at work, unemployment insurance, retirement benefit, invalidity and death benefit. Contributions are calculated as a percentage of gross income and are deducted at source by the employer. Social security contributions by the employee are around 6%. The total contribution is around 30% – a very large figure that influences employment practices.

Public holidays

The government allows 14 national and local public holidays a year, more than any other country in Europe. Of these two are regional or municipal holidays to celebrate dates of local importance. All public offices, banks and post offices are closed on public holidays. In addition most regions and towns have their own carnival and fiesta days.

Annual holidays

Under law a full-time employee is entitled to a minimum of 23 working days' paid annual holiday. When both annual and public holidays are taken into account, Spain has the greatest number of holidays of any EU country.

August is the traditional month for summer holidays, with many businesses closing down entirely. Some businesses close for two weeks over Christmas and New Year and many restaurants for the month of February.

Dismissal and redundancy

In addition to reasons such as mutual agreement, death, expiration of the contractual term and retirement, an employment contract can be collectively terminated for technological and economic reasons, and individually for objective or disciplinary reasons.

An employee can be made redundant on technological and economic grounds only in relation to the collective restructuring of a company's workforce. Technological and economic causes are legally defined terms, when the employer may decide dismissal unilaterally.

Objective reasons for dismissal include employee ineptitude and the inability to adapt to technological change. Legal grounds for dismissal for disciplinary reasons include insubordination or disobedience, repeated absenteeism or lateness, physical or verbal abuse, fraud, disloyalty or abuse of confidence, poor performance, carrying on business on his own account for a third party without the consent of the employer, and habitual drug or alcohol abuse.

An employee dismissed for objective or disciplinary reasons may challenge the decision in the labour courts.

THE BLACK ECONOMY

Illegal working is common in Italy, Spain and neighbouring Morocco. The black economy (*economía sumergida*) or the cash-for-services labour market is a significant proportion of the country's generated wealth.

What causes this situation?

- Influxes of illegal Moroccan immigrants seeking to better themselves in Spain are keen to accept low cash payments for unskilled work.

- It is illegal for non-EU nationals to work in Spain without a work permit (the application is by the employer). Unscrupulous employers bypass this procedure and use this labour to pay low wages for long hours in poor working conditions This occurs in industries that traditionally employ casual labour, such as building, farming and food service.

◆ Illegal working avoids the payment of additional employment on-costs (particularly social security and IVA payments – see p. 80). This can make the difference between a fair product price and one too expensive, or the difference between profit and loss.

◆ Many casual, seasonal workers – or indeed full-time workers – choose to work illegally. They do not pay tax or social security contributions and while no entitlement to state benefits are available for work injury, health care, unemployment benefit or pension their view is that these are small penalties for not having to pay a hefty social security charge.

HAVING YOUR OWN BUSINESS

What business?

Spain is traditionally a country of small companies and sole traders. There are nearly two million families running businesses employing about 75% of the working population.

The majority of businesses established by foreigners in Spain are linked to the leisure and catering industries or to property sales. Why? The answer is twofold: low entry capital cost and providing a service in one's mother tongue. Figure 5 outlines the steps involved.

People choose to be self-employed for the lifestyle and freedom it affords but small businesses in Spain often exist on a shoestring with owners working extremely long hours, particularly those running bars or restaurants. Many foreigners start businesses in Spain with little research, little business acumen, no knowledge, no capital and no linguistic ability. It is asking for trouble.

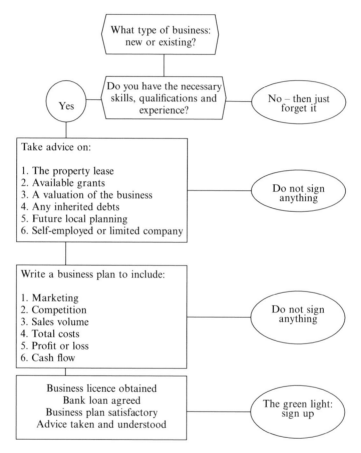

Figure 5. Setting up your own business

Before establishing a business it is important to obtain legal advice to avoid breaking the law, to understand the rules and regulations and to take advantage of tax benefits. This advice can be obtained from a lawyer (*abogado*), an accountant (*asesor fiscal*) or a *gestor*.

'If man can imagine something, then man can do it' are good words from a management guru. However, businesses operated by foreigners in Spain are a lot simpler. They include:

- bookshops and lending libraries
- business and secretarial services
- car sales – usually second-hand
- caravan and camping sites
- catering – bars, cafés and restaurants
- computer sales and service
- construction work
- discotheques and nightclubs
- English or Spanish language schools, translation and interpreting
- estate agents and holiday letting
- hairdressing
- hotels, guesthouses and other accommodation
- kennels and catteries
- satellite television installation
- second-hand furniture stores.
- shops
- sports centres and tuition.

Buying an existing business
- It is easier to buy an existing business than it is to start a new one.

- An established business is less of a risk than starting something new.

- Finding an existing business that is a good going concern is not easy.

- People do not sell a thriving business without a good reason.

- Traditional Spanish businesses are usually passed down within the family.

- What is the reason for selling? Is there a hidden motive?

- Check at the local planning office for anything that may affect the business.

- Have two independent valuations been obtained?

- It is essential to take legal advice regarding the lease.

- Ensure sales turnover and profit claims can be substantiated.

- Remember when buying a business property in Spain that all debts against the property are automatically transferred to the new owner.

- It is important to obtain all necessary licences before signing a lease or purchase contract.

Starting a new business

- Is there a business plan in existence?

- Most people are too optimistic about the prospects of a new business.

- Lack of capital is the most common reason for business failure.

- All banks are wary of lending to a new business.

- Borrowing money? Is it the euro, the dollar or the pound?

- When starting a retail business, people traffic is governed by location.

- Is access to motorways and rail links important?

- Is access to a popular tourist area or local attractions important?

- Are any housing developments or new shopping centres planned nearby?

GETTING STARTED

What type of company

An EU national or a permanent resident with an NIE and *residencia* can be self-employed (*trabajador autónomo*) or work as a sole trader (*empresa individual*). Members of some professions and trades must possess professional qualifications recognised in Spain, e.g. medical practitioners must have qualifications accepted by the medical college in the province where they intend to practise and must also show good standing with their professional authorities back home.

A self-employed person does not have the protection of a limited company should the business fail. It may be advantageous to operate as a limited company, but 'limited companies' cannot be purchased off the shelf. A *gestor* can do this, but it usually takes some time.

A business may assume various legal titles. Most small businesspeople operate as sole traders and must register with the appropriate trade association and pay a small entrance fee and a monthly subscription. A small company is usually a private limited company (*sociedad de responsabilidad limitada*), designated SL. It is the simplest and most common form of limited company and does not have any public shares. A large limited company is a public company (*sociedad anónima*) designated SA which is similar to a British Plc or an American Inc. To form an SA requires a minimum of share capital and at least 50 employees and one director.

Opening licence

A business having premises such as a shop, workshop or offices requires an opening licence (*licencia de apertura*) from the local council before starting.

If a business is likely to inconvenience the local community, for example through noise from a bar or discotheque, the council will insist on certain requirements before granting the opening licence. A licence application is not necessary if the business premises are to be used for the same purpose as previously.

A licence issued for a business owned by a non-EU national may be conditional on the employment of a minimum number of EU citizens.

Grants

Investment incentives are available from the Spanish government and the EU. Incentives include investment subsidies, tax relief, low-interest or interest-free loans, social security rebates and reduced local taxes during the start-up period. There are also regional government incentives for investment in economic promotion zones, declining industrial zones and urgent re-industrialisation zones.

CASE STUDY

Renting premises

Question

I rented some premises with the idea of opening a bar. After a few months I was informed by the town hall that they would not be granting a licence as the premises did not comply with the necessary conditions for this kind of activity.

I contacted the landlord and advised him of the situation. He stated he had no intention of cancelling the contract and I must continue to pay him the money as stipulated in the contract. What do I do?

Answer

There are three situations in which the contract may be cancelled:

1. by mutual agreement;
2. the wording in the contract allows you to do so;
3. by a judicial sentence that declares the contract cancelled.

It may be that in this case there is no alternative but to go to court and request the judge to declare the contract null and void. But if you rented the premises with the clear intention of opening a bar, this is clearly stated in the contract and you were prevented from doing so by a ruling from the town hall then the contract has no substance and can be cancelled in accordance with article 1091 of the Spanish Civil Code and confirmed by the Supreme Court.

It is usual, however, to mention in a contract that the landlord is not responsible for obtaining a license and this would weaken your position. Taking legal advice before signing anything is important.

BUSINESS ON-COSTS

Social security
All self-employed people and businesses must register with the social security scheme. The cost of social security contributions for the self-employed is higher than for employees and the benefits less. This astronomical cost simply encourages illegal working. Why pay around €230 per month for a benefit that may be rarely used? This is a good example of the black economy being inadvertently influenced by the state.

Impuesto sobre actividades economicas (IAE)
All self-employed people and businesses must register at the Hacienda to pay a tax known as IAE. It is payable if business turnover exceeds €600,000 per year. What is it? They say it is a tax on economic activities. The high sales threshold is designed to help small and medium businesses financially. This tax was formerly paid to the town hall.

Impuesto sobre el valor añadido (IVA)
All self-employed people and businesses must register for valued added tax (IVA) and levy this tax on all services or goods.

Taxation
Small businesses pay an estimated quarterly tax with a refund made, or an additional payment demanded, at the end of the tax year. Limited companies must file corporate tax returns to the provincial tax headquarters in the area where the business is registered. Various returns must be made including corporation tax, personal

income tax, income tax of sole proprietors and value added tax.

SUMMARY

◆ The main requirement for someone working in Spain is to master the language.

◆ Spanish employers can be sharp. Working for ex-pats offers no extra security.

◆ There are opportunities for casual, seasonal, part-time or full-time work.

◆ Teaching English is a major employment opportunity. The British Council is strong in this field.

◆ Like all countries, Spain too has a contract of employment. Pay is low, fringe benefits are good but social security payments cost a lot.

◆ The black economy is rife. Illegal immigrants, casual work and high social security payments encourage this.

◆ Having your own business is often a dream but skill, knowledge and capital are required.

◆ Getting started means an opening licence, setting up some form of business and getting professional advice.

Deciding Where to Go and Stay

DECIDING WHERE TO GO

Northern Europeans, when considering Spain, tend to favour an area near or just a few kilometres from the sea. Consequently, in order to describe the country, we will divide Spain into costal areas.

- ◆ Northern Spain running from west to east and facing the Atlantic Ocean comprises the six *comunidades* of Galicia, Asturias, Cantabria, the Basque Country, Navarra and La Rioja.

- ◆ Eastern Spain comprises Aragon which faces the Pyrenees and runs from north to south, and Catalonia, Valencia and Murcia all of which face the Eastern Mediterranean embracing well known places such as the Costa Brava, the Costa Dorada, the Costa Azahar and the universally acknowledged Costa Blanca.

- ◆ Southern Spain comprises only one *comunidade*, the largest and best known, Andalucia, which faces in two directions: the Costa del Sol which faces the Mediterranean and the Costa de la Luz which faces the Atlantic Ocean.

- ◆ In the heart of the country lies central Spain with the four *comunidades* of Madrid, Castilla-la-Mancha, Extremadura and Castilla y León.

◆ Spain's Islands comprise the popular Balearics in the east Mediterranean and the Canaries set to the south-west in the warm waters of the Atlantic.

Green Northern Spain

Increasing numbers of people are discovering the deep green landscapes, the solitude of the mountains and the quiet sandy beaches of Northern Spain. The Atlantic coast from the Portuguese border to the Pyrenees is often scenic but no more so than the cliffs of Galicia and the Picos mountains. Inland the mild but wet climate has created lush green meadows and broad-leaved forests.

Galicia, to the west, has as its centrepiece the beautiful old city of Santiago de Compostela. Surrounded by forest-covered hills, the way of life seems to have changed little in centuries.

To the east in Asturias and Cantabria, the most obvious attraction is the group of mountains called the Picos de Europa, which straddles the two communities. These mountains, set in a national park, offer excellent rock climbing and good hiking, but in winter, when covered in snow, are extremely dangerous.

Further east lies the Basque Country, Navarra and La Rioja, a green hilly region offering the diverse sporting attractions of the Pyrenees. It includes the fine city of San Sebastian gloriously situated on a neat shell-shaped bay, now recognised as an elegant and fashionable resort and renowned for its great summer arts festivals – jazz, classical music and film. It is also home to the Basques, a group suppressed under Franco's reign, but since the arrival of democracy they have had their own Parliament and their own police force. Although always wishing for more, they have great autonomy over their own affairs.

Some people say this region is like Scotland, Ireland, Wales and England rolled into one. It is mild, wet and definitely green – just like being at home but with a different culture.

Diverse Eastern Spain

This is a large area encompassing Aragon, Catalonia, Valencia and Murcia. It embraces Barcelona, the eastern Pyrenees, and four Costas – Brava, Dorada, Azahar and Blanca.

Barcelona is unquestionably a fine place. One of the Mediterranean's busiest ports, it is much more than the capital of Catalonia. Culturally, commercially and in sport it not only rivals Madrid but also rightfully considers itself on a par with the greatest European cities. The success of the Olympic Games confirmed this to the world. It is always open to outside influences because of its location not too far from the French border. Las Ramblas is the most famous street in Spain. It is busy round the clock, especially in the evenings and at weekends. News stands, caged birds, flower stalls, tarot readers, musicians and mime artists throng the wide, tree-shaded, central walkway.

The northern borders of the *comunidades* of Aragon and Catalonia butt onto the Pyrenees and France. Catalonia additionally faces east to the Mediterranean giving us the first taste of two Costas – Brava and Dorada.

Aragon stretches almost half the length of Spain and is bisected by the Ebro, one of the country's longest rivers. It takes in a wide variety of scenery, from the snow-capped mountains of the Ordesa National Park in the Pyrenees to the dry plains of the interior. The major cities are Teruel and the capital Zaragoza, Spain's fifth largest city. The climate of the region varies as much as the landscape with the winters long and harsh and the summers very hot. Northern Europeans rarely settle in Aragon unless they have a love affair with the Pyrenees.

Catalonia presents an altogether different picture – a proud nation within a nation with its own language, Catalán, which has all but replaced Spanish in place names and on road signs throughout the region. Eight million people speak the language, now fully recovered from the ban it suffered under Franco's dictatorship. Its major cities are Taragona and, of course, Barcelona, the region's capital.

In the 1960s the rugged Costa Brava (Wild Coast) became one of Europe's first mass package holiday destinations. Tourism quickly followed to the long sandy stretches of the Costa Dorada (Golden Coast).

The *comunidades* of Valencia and Murcia have as their coastal region the more popularly known Costa del Azahar (Orange Blossom) and the Costa Blanca (White Coast). This area is distinguished by its fine climate. The principal holiday resorts are Benidorm, Torrevieja and Mar Menor. It has fine commercial centres at Valencia, Spain's third largest city, Alicante, the main city on the Costa Blanca, Cartagena, a former naval base, and of course Murcia, a lively university city.

Having warmer winters than the Costa Brava but being cheaper and less fashionable than the Costa del Sol, the Costa Blanca occupies a prime stretch of Mediterranean coastline with Alicante's airport and main line railway station a major communication hub. Long sandy beaches, in places lined with hotels and apartment blocks, are a feature of the area.

Andalucia – Southern Spain

So to Andalucia, a large area extending across the south of the country incorporating the deserts of Almeria, the wetlands of Donana, the snow capped peaks of the Sierra Nevada and the beaches of the Costa del Sol. It is the home of many white-walled villages. The capital Seville rivals Barcelona for fine city living.

El Arenal, a district of Seville, was once home to an ammunition factory and artillery headquarters but now the atmosphere is set by the city's majestic bullring called the *Plaza de Toros de la Maestranza*. During the bullfighting season the bars and restaurants are packed, but for the rest of the year many people on boat trips enjoy the wide Quadalquivir River. The *barrio* of Santa Cruz is a district of Seville. It was the old Jewish quarter, a warren of white alleyways and flower-decked patios, now representing Seville at its most romantic and compact.

The maze of narrow streets hides *tapas* bars, plazas and upmarket residences. Ornamental orange trees line the streets, their bittersweet tasting fruit suitable for making marmalade. It was, however, Expo '92, which focused world attention on Seville, where over one hundred countries were represented in the many pavilions which displayed scientific, technological and cultural exhibits.

To the north lies Almeria. It is a major supplier of fruit and vegetables to the rest of Europe. The area is noted for Europe's only desert, the Trabernas, made famous as the location for Spaghetti Westerns such as *The Good, the Bad and the Ugly*, starring Clint Eastwood.

The Costa del Sol may be one of the most overdeveloped strips of coastline in the world, but thanks to 300 days of sunshine per year this area of Spain is home to many. It boasts the jet set sophistication of Marbella and has over 30 golf courses lying just inland. There are many resorts aimed at the mass tourist market, but some of the older developments just south of Málaga have a tired, well-worn look, with planners now facing the difficult task of possible demolition.

The highlight of the area is unquestionably Marbella, a stylish resort with Puerto Banus as its ostentatious marina. Expensive shops, restaurants and glittering nightlife reflect the wealth of its inhabitants and visitors. Close behind is the up and coming Sotogrande, an exclusive resort of luxury villas with a marina and golf course. Estepona is quieter, not so built-up and not attached to the long concrete strip that unfortunately is a characteristic of this Costa. Málaga is another fine city with a thriving port. Its new shopping centre presents an interesting blend of the old and the new.

A few miles inland from the coast at Málaga a different Spain opens up with lots of greenery and many thousands of classical white houses covering the rounded slopes. Even small towns are cut into the contours of the landscape. Instead of settling on the fertile plains, some Andalucians chose to live in fortified hilltop towns now known as *pueblos blancos* (white towns) whitewashed in the Moorish tradition and today working agricultural villages. Ronda is the best known.

Granada and Córdoba are old Moorish cities. The benefits of hiking and skiing in the nearby Sierra Nevada mountains compensate a little for the cold winters and baking hot summers.

Costa de la Luz, the Coast of Light, is situated to the west of Gibraltar facing the Atlantic. Spain's southernmost tip is an unspoilt, windswept stretch of coast characterised by strong pure light – hence its name. Other than Cádiz, which is almost entirely surrounded by water, Jerez, the capital of sherry production, the Donana National Park, an area of wetlands, sand dunes and marshland, the region has little to commend it.

Vast central Spain

The vast central plateau is covered in dry dusty plains and large rolling fields. Given the attractions of the Costas and the Islands it is not an area where many Europeans settle.

It is a place of work. Long straight roads and vast fields devoted to wheat, sunflowers and the grape dominate the region. It is remote and of stunning beauty, suitable for those engaged in agriculture or for those who want to get well off the beaten track, going back to nature in old rural Spain.

Situated in the centre of the country is the capital. Madrid is a city of over three million people and a crossroads for rail, road and air travel. Its altitude of 660 meters gives rise to a classic temperature profile of cold winters and hot summers, making spring and autumn the best times to visit. Those who can escape from Madrid during August make for the cooler north or south to the Mediterranean.

Despite the climate the capital city has developed its own unique personality. It boasts the *Parque del Retiro*, a world famous area of leafy paths and avenues, a royal palace and grand public squares. Its museums are filled with Spain's historic treasures. Madrid is a city that offers the best in shopping facilities. The latest designer clothes are sold in elegant upmarket stores. There are food markets throughout the city and the centuries-old *Rastro*, open every Sunday, is one of the world's greatest flea markets.

The holiday islands

Spain's two groups of islands lie in separate seas. The Balearics are in the Mediterranean and the Canaries in the Atlantic, off the African coast. The islands, blessed with a warm climate, good beaches and clear waters, are visited by hundreds of thousands of people each year.

Often associated with mass inexpensive tourism the Balearics have something for everyone. For those turning their backs on the bustle of coastal resorts with all their attractions, the countryside and old towns lie relatively undisturbed. The Balearics have white villages, wooded hills and caves. Mallorca, a culturally rich island, has mountains to go with the sea and shore. Ibiza is known for its nightlife. Menorca and Formentera are quieter, more tranquil.

Mallorca is a good choice. Access is usually by air, but there are also excellent ferry services from Barcelona, Valencia, Alicante or Denia. The west coast, from Andratx to Pollenca and the Gallic influence of Soller, is particularly attractive. Palma, the capital, is a clean, bustling city.

The Canary Islands are poised on the edge of the tropics west of Morocco. They enjoy plentiful sunshine and are pleasantly cooled by the trade winds. The Canaries have extraordinary volcanic landscapes unlike any other part of Spain. The scenery ranges from lava desert to forest, from sand dunes to volcanic mountains. There are seven islands. Tenerife, Gran Canaria and Lanzarote are the largest.

Mount Teide, an awesome sight and the highest mountain in Spain, dominates Tenerife. Volcanic material forms a wilderness of weathered, mineral tinted rocks. A single road passes through the area, passing a hotel, cable car station and a visitors' centre. Los Cristianos is an old fishing port, which has developed into a pleasant town along the foothills of a barren landscape.

Las Palmas the capital of Gran Canaria is another fine city. Playa del Inglés is a holiday area of high-rise hotel and apartment blocks best avoided. Puerto Rico and Puerto del Morgan on the other hand are attractive, unique, pretty places, quite the opposite of the brash concrete holiday resorts.

A ROOF OVER YOUR HEAD

Hotels
Tourism is a vital industry for Spain and has resulted in thousands of hotels of all grades. Some examples of hotel chains and their websites can be found in Appendix 11. Hotels are government regulated. They must fulfil certain requirements according to their star rating. A five-star hotel will have air conditioning in all public rooms and bedrooms, central heating and all bedrooms will have fully furnished bathrooms. *Paradores* (see below) are a good example of this. Three- or four-star hotels are good quality. One- and two-star hotels will have central heating but not all bedrooms will be en suite.

An unusual fact! With the recent construction of four new macro hotels, Benidorm is currently third behind London and Paris in offering tourist accommodation – and cheaper. The newly opened Gran Hotel Bali is the tallest building in Spain at 210 metres and the tallest hotel in Europe. The Bali's figures are impressive. It employs 278 people, has 776 rooms with 1,608 beds, a convention hall with assembly rooms for 3,000 people and restaurants for 1,000.

Interested in rooms at a particular hotel?

◆ Do they have rooms? – *¿Hay habitaciónes?*

◆ For an individual room ask for *una habitación individual*. It may well be that there are two single beds in the room, but the charge will only be for one.

◆ Intending to share a room? Ask for a *una habitación doble*, which will be a room with two single beds.

◆ If you want a double bed, ask for *una habitación con cama matrimonial* (a room with a double bed).

◆ A room with a bath is *una habitación con baño*, and one with a shower is *una habitación con ducha*.

Paradores

The Spanish tourist industry is proud of its unique network of 86 hotels called *paradores*. They range from three- to five-star, the majority of which are restored historic monuments such as castles, monasteries, convents or palaces. Great care has been taken to preserve their decor and distinctive characteristics while converting them into high-quality modern hotels. Even the modern purpose-designed *paradores* reflect regional styles and have unique decor and furnishing. Their restaurants, too, pride themselves on regional cuisine and wine. Travelling around Spain staying in *paradores* is a special way of seeing the country.

◆ There is a high standard of service and cleanliness.

◆ The cuisine is excellent, normally to international standards and caters for all tastes.

- The buildings are usually interesting and the facilities are modern.

- They are frequently located in beauty spots which are off the beaten track.

- They are expensive.

Balneario (spa)

There are numerous spas. They take you back to the nineteenth century with a leisurely way of life and treatments which range from a rest cure to a full medical twice daily programme controlled by doctors and staff. Fourteen of Spain's 17 regions have spas. They can be like expensive hotels. *Te enseñamos el poder del agua thermal* (We teach you the power of the thermal waters).

The history of spas is interesting for Spain was once rich in medicinal baths and spas which have always been a strong Mediterranean tradition. Most have fallen into decay but a few of these ancient baths still survive in Granada, Jaen, Córdoba, Ronda and, surprisingly, in Gibraltar. The Moors still practise the art of bathing for pleasure in their home country of Morocco with each town having several public baths known as *hammams*. Of course it was these peaceful invaders who built and developed the spas of Spain.

Organised bathing was firstly segregated into male and female areas and then into three areas of cold, warm and hot. The cold room was for undressing, clothes being replaced with towels, bathrobes and slippers. The warm room would have pools. The hot room was rather like today's sauna.

By the side of each room was an area to rest where attendants would tend to all the needs of the bathers. Barbers and masseurs fussed around performing unimaginable duties while others stoked the wood-burning fires or cleaned the area. The bathers lounged, relaxed, gossiped or did some business. It was decadence, wealth and power for many of the bathers were very rich.

Hostales and pensiones

They are usually defined by the letters MS or P on a blue background outside the establishment. They are more modest forms of accommodation but, like hotels, they are graded according to the facilities offered. The star rating is based on facilities so a two- or three-star hostel can be better in terms of furnishing than a low-rated hotel. They are good value for money.

Guesthouse

The most basic form of accommodation consisting of rooms with only a simple bed and washbasin is to be found in *fondas* or *casas de huespedes*, which are both forms of guesthouse or lodgings. They can be identified by signs with the letters F or CM in white letters on a blue background and are usually to be found in the older sections of a town.

Farmhouses and casa rurales

This accommodation offers a chance to see rural life without losing the basic comforts of a hotel. The houses are not necessarily in the country – indeed, the majority are in villages. Government money has been granted for the purpose of improving a home or a house not in use in order to make it suitable for receiving visitors. This has had the effect of conserving and modernising country dwellings and thus offering the possibility of holidays away from the traditional centres of tourist activity.

Wayside inns

Many wayside restaurants, often called *ventas*, have accommodation, which they advertise with the sign *camas* (beds). If the sign is not visible but the establishment looks large enough to have rooms above the restaurant ask *¿Hay camas?* (Are there beds?). These places are useful on a long drive, if there is a need for a meal and an overnight stop, without having to divert to search the nearest town or village.

Campsites

Spain has hundreds of registered campsites where a tent can be pitched or caravan parked. These sites can be found close to major cities, next to beaches, by rivers and lakes and throughout the whole of Spain. Considering the range of facilities offered by most sites, camping is particularly good value. Prime sites have showers, launderette facilities, bars, restaurants, first aid/medical facilities, shops, a swimming pool, telephones, post boxes, safes for valuables, electric and water supplies for caravans and a range of sporting facilities.

Off-site camping is permitted in Spain, subject to the permission of the landowner, but not in the mountains or on beaches.

Timeshare

A classic timeshare investment is where the co-owner pays a sum of money which is an entitlement to use a specified property for a number of weeks at a certain time of year. Additionally there is an annual fee for the management and upkeep of the property. The main principal of timeshare is that it gives quality accommodation for less than the equivalent hotel rate.

It is, however, an industry that has a bad reputation for unscrupulous practices. This is changing. Spain introduced timeshare regulations in 1999. The highlights are:

◆ restrictions on high-pressure selling tactics in public places and tourist spots;

◆ the introduction of a cooling-off period of ten days during which the buyer can withdraw from the contract with no penalty;

◆ the need to have written information supplied in the mother tongue of the buyer;

◆ Spanish law governing contract disputes.

Holiday homes

Anyone looking for a holiday home will invariably come across the town of Torrevieja, the fastest expanding town in Spain where, since the mid-80s, houses have been built at a prodigious rate. In the last ten years the town's registered population grew by a staggering 135%. In the next five years new homes are planned at the rate of 6,000 units per year. What is the attraction? Properties in Torrevieja are cheap, the climate excellent and communications good. The downside? There is a profusion of Irish bars and Chinese restaurants, and it boasts Spain's first Anne Summers sex shop. In summer it is wall to wall with people, the beaches are packed and the restaurants are full. In winter, the white urbanisations are mostly uninhabited.

DID YOU KNOW?
Cave dwellers

In Andalucia there are thousands of cave dwellers. The structure of the soil at Guadix near Granada means that these caves can be excavated and turned into homes. They are not natural caves. Many have eight rooms, an electricity supply, sewage disposal, television and garage. They may house animals. They can be two storeys high, be converted into bars, restaurants, discos or churches. They are quiet, do not leak or collapse, have a constant temperature of 17 degrees all year round and can be easily modified.

A cave home can be bought and sold in the normal way. As the younger Spaniards leave the caves to work in the town or city so demand has decreased and therefore cave houses are very cheap.

Cave houses have become tourist attractions. Government subsidies are available to preserve them. Coach tours are commonplace. 'Rent-a-cave' is a fact. *Cuevas Pedro Antonio de Alarcón* is a hotel cave complex in Guadix, with richly furnished rooms, all mod cons and excellent food.

PROPERTY RENTAL

Holiday rental

There are many self-catering properties for rent in Spain. Properties have been built for that purpose or are available from absentee owners. They will mainly be apartments near the sea, a golf course or a villa in the mountains. Many detached villas with a swimming pool or rustic country houses are also available through upmarket letting agents.

Short-term holiday rental companies can advertise their wares more effectively through a website than by thousands of very expensive brochures. Information can be assimilated very quickly making the web ideal for accessing the up-to-date availability of any holiday rental. Viewing the alternatives on a screen, checking price and availability, booking and paying by credit card are but a few clicks away. E-commerce is rapidly taking over as the most effective method of booking a holiday rental.

Holiday rental contracts are called *arrienda de temporada*. The property is furnished. The straightforward, standard contract is in Spanish or in English. With a returnable deposit required to cover any damages caused by the temporary tenant, the contract is for a specific period of time at a stated price. The renewal of the contract is at the agent's or landlord's discretion.

Long-term rental
Properties available for long-term rental are found mainly, but not exclusively, in the city. They can be furnished or unfurnished. It is an expensive method of accommodation only for those with special needs. Over a five-year period it is obviously cheaper to buy and then sell than it is to rent.

Like most countries Spain has its letting law. It is called *Ley de Arrendamientos Urbanos* and came into force in

1995. The contract for a long-term rental is called *arrienda de vivienda*. The law provides for long-term rentals to be of five years' duration thus giving the tenant a degree of security. If the landlord offers a contract of three years' duration, which is accepted, and then the tenant wishes to stay on for another two years it is automatically renewed on the same terms. If the tenant wishes to leave after three years then the contract is terminated.

Annual rent increases in line with inflation take place during the contracted term. A new level of rent is set at the commencement of a new contract.

SUMMARY

- There are many places to stay. The lush green fields and mountains of northern Spain remind people of home. Barcelona and the Costa Blanca are prime locations. Many love Andalucia and the Costa del Sol. Time stands still in central Spain. Is it the Islands that hold an attraction?

- Hotels, *paradores* and *hostales* are major stopping points to rest and eat.

- Spain also has spas, guesthouses, inns, cottages, good campsites and, of course, timeshares.

- Consider the purchase of a holiday home – thousands of people do. Or perhaps a cave house!

- Property rental is now mainly advertised through e-commerce. The contract is important, particularly for a long-term rental.

7

Buying a Property

CONSIDERING THE PROS AND CONS OF EACH HOUSE TYPE

Apartment

Choosing to live in an apartment offers easy living in secure surroundings. In order to sell quickly they are always built to a high standard, with outside balconies included. Some basic economy flats exist in large cities where low-cost living is a priority. Living in an apartment will probably mean Spanish neighbours. Nice people they may well be, but they tend to be noisy and have a different 'body clock' to other nationalities. Normal behaviour is to rise late and go to bed at midnight or after.

Linked, terraced and town houses

These houses are on two levels with a third floor/roof utilised as a solarium. They are cheap, easy to resell but lack privacy. Town houses are available new, but can also be older refurbished traditional properties in the narrow streets of a Spanish town where car parking is a problem.

Corner properties

Corner housing is most utilised in the form of a duplex design (a house on two levels with an internal staircase) but can also apply to single-level homes. It is a cheap form of building having fewer external walls. Services, although individual to each home, do have some common elements. They are noisy, but their main function is holiday homes, with neighbours meeting only on rare occasions.

Detached
These properties offer privacy at the expense of security. They can be expensive. Built to an individual design they are sometimes perched precariously on cutaway hillsides, so much so that insurance companies can charge a premium. Windswept plots make dust a perpetual irritant. Even with some disadvantages a detached property is desirable, particularly one that overlooks the sea or the mountains or even a lush green golf course.

Traditional homes
Older Spanish houses are in abundance. In most cases they have been modernised or rebuilt. In the country they are called *fincas*. A refurbished town house is in many respects an ideal property since it gives easy access to the town with the benefits of living in new modern surroundings.

The classic is a *finca rustica*, located in the country. With determination and money rebuilding an old crumbling building into an individual, personalised property of pride and charm can be an exciting project.

Urbanisations
Life on an urbanisation is popular whatever the type of house. Sitting by the swimming pool meeting new continental friends, passing the time of day with a glass of wine in hand, is an agreeable way of life. Behaviour standards need to be set. An urbanisation is a community by itself where the level is set by the standard of the lowest.

Community property

What is a community property? The answer is one that involves homes with a shared element. An example would be apartments, or a grouping of individual homes. Urbanisations have a shared element in the swimming pool or gardens. Apartments have a shared element in the lift. Detached properties may have a common access road.

The cost of maintaining these elements is shared between the owners. The most expensive is normally the swimming pool, followed by gardens and satellite TV. Spanish council services are limited, with elements such as street cleaning being part of the community costs.

The *communidad de propietarios* can be run by an independent company on behalf of the owners or, in a well-organised community, by the owners themselves. Germans have a talent for this, the Spanish an eye for detail while the Scandinavians are laid back. The British and Irish seem happy to leave it to others.

New or resale

When moving to Spain most people prefer to buy a new property. It is rather like buying a car. Why buy second-hand if you can buy new? A resale property is slightly more expensive, after all drives have been laid, gardens are mature and it often comes with furniture and fittings. A resale property built within the last ten years may still carry a guarantee. It can be of good value. In some, now overdeveloped, parts of Spain it is the only type of property available.

Living by the sea

This is a pleasant experience with cool afternoon breezes taking the sting out of the searing summer heat. But nearly all Mediterranean towns are tourist areas. In July and August with temperatures always in excess of 30 degrees, people pour in on package holidays. Spaniards too decide to have their summer holiday and rush to the coast in thousands from the torrid heat of the big cities. For two frustrating months the beaches are packed, the roads jammed, car parks full and tempers frayed.

Living in the country

Living in the country has many attractions. It is living in the real Spain. It is peaceful with privacy assured. Neighbours, although far apart, are normally friendly. Large plots of land enable the growing of oranges, lemons, olives or almonds. Some of these properties have no electricity, no water, no sewage disposal, no gas and no telephone. The lack of these facilities can be overcome by other means.

Which direction?

There is a bay at Calpe with a hilly headland jutting out eastwards to sea. Houses have been built on this hill. They face north. They are cold houses as they get little direct sun. Individual houses, a terraced row, or apartments facing north or north-east all suffer from the same fate – little sun in the summer months and consequently quite cool inside. For year round living it is better to choose a property facing to the South. For a summer holiday home it is not so important.

The magic of position

What do we really want when buying a house? Is it a property close to the sea, overlooking a golf course, with easy access to the countryside, a town and an airport? Is it to be new, white, set in a large plot of land? Do restaurants and pubs, hospitals, doctors and dentists have to be close by? Are neighbours only to be British, Irish and the rather pleasant Dutch?

No, not really! What we do is to set a number of priorities, which are usually the price, the number of bedrooms, the type of house and the location. Then we look for *position*.

The three Ps beloved by property consultants are Position, Position and Position. It is that little magic that makes a property unique and easy to sell.

THE PEOPLE INVOLVED IN BUYING

The agent

- A good agent is one who can offer a wide variety of properties for sale.

- Greater security is offered by dealing with an agent who is professionally qualified or belongs to a professional organisation.

- For first-time buyers, uncertain of the laws and customs of the country, a good agent will give additional assistance during the difficult moving-in stage.

Agents dealing in Spanish property do take a high commission. The lowest start at around 3% but the average is 10%. When selling a *finca* it can be 25%. How do they justify such exorbitant charges? Their answer is ambiguous, making reference to high advertising costs, commissions due in two countries and complex transactions involving different nationalities.

The commission rate for selling a new house on behalf of a builder is usually fixed at around 10%. If a number of agents are selling the same properties they may compete with each other discounting their commission by offering furniture packages to prospective purchasers.

A different commission structure operates for the sale of a second-hand property, commonly termed a resale property. In some cases the agent operates on a fixed commission, but it is more customary for the following arrangement:

- The agent asks the seller the price he wishes for the property.

- He advertises and negotiates the sale of the property at another, higher price.

- The difference between the two prices is the agent's commission, which is rarely less than 10%, more likely to be 15% and can in special cases reach 25%.

- This pricing structure gives rise to considerable animosity. It is compounded when buyer and seller seldom meet, creating an atmosphere of mistrust in relation to the commercial motives of the agent.

The *abogado* (solicitor)

It is important to remember that the appointment of a legal representative is principally to protect the buyer. The agent is working for the seller. Rather like many other aspects of daily life, it is a system of checks and balances. But let us be clear at the outset. The Spanish system of house conveyancing is different. You are not dealing with solicitors who draw up and exchange contracts on completion.

So what does the *abogado* do? The *abogado*:

- draws up a contract should they be asked to do so;

- helps complete the conveyance of the property;

- provides help and guidance on legal matters, principally the content of the contract and payment methods;

- makes arrangements to obtain and receive a power of attorney should this be necessary if the parties will not be available to sign the *escritura* (see below);

- obtains an NIE number so that a client's personal identification is by name and also number.

- makes arrangements for signing the *escritura* and final property payments.

The bank

A bank may be recommended by a friend, an agent or the *abogado*, or be linked with a bank back home. Here are some recommended criteria for selecting a bank.

◆ Some staff, preferably the manager, should speak English.

◆ In order to have access to major services such as mortgages and investments, the bank should be a major player in the Spanish marketplace.

◆ Money transferred into Spain for the purchase of a property will come through the clearing bank system. The bank back home and the Spanish bank should both be main branches to prevent delays in money transfer.

Need a mortgage? The Spanish bank is a provider. Need a short-term bridging loan? Forget it. These two statements demonstrate a difference in attitude towards borrowing money. A loan is seen for business and a mortgage for home finance, with the two kept strictly separate.

The *notario*

In Spain all deeds for properties are drawn up by public notaries who are appointed by the government. They are qualified lawyers who have additionally studied to become notaries. They are very important people in the Spanish community, responsible for legalising many documents including the power of attorney, drawing up wills, certifying copies of passports and, most importantly, approving the deed of a property, known in Spain as the *escritura*.

The *escritura* is signed and witnessed by the *notario* in the presence of the seller(s) and the purchaser(s) unless any party has utilised the power of attorney to excuse their own presence. The *notario*'s duty is to:

- check the name of the titleholder and whether there are any charges or encumbrances against the property;

- check the contents of the *escritura*;

- ensure the *escritura* is read to the purchaser(s) prior to signing;

- check that both parties have been advised of their legal obligations;

- certify the *escritura* has been signed and the money paid.

The *notario* represents the state. He does not guarantee or verify statements or check the contractual terms. He protects the interests of the buyer or seller by pointing out any pitfalls, by offering advice on legal points and volunteering information.

The end product of a visit to the *notario* is the *escritura*. It is a hard-backed copy of the deed, which is covered in official stamps, signatures and writing. It is typed on thick, numbered paper. It is an impressive document produced to a standard format.

The gestor

A *gestor* acts as an intermediary between Spanish officialdom and the general public being a registered agent dealing with government departments. It says much about the Spanish way of life that such a person is necessary to deal with its wearisome bureaucracy. What do they do? For the Spanish they simply deal with the complicated mass of paperwork. For foreigners they do the same, in a country where the language barrier, a new culture and different procedures can cause additional problems. The tasks covered by the *gestor* are:

◆ application for residency;

◆ entry into the Spanish health system;

◆ dealing with the payment of car tax, car transfer tax and other car related matters;

◆ payment of income and wealth taxes;

◆ if required, help in setting up a new business.

Avoiding problems

Problems associated with purchasing a property abroad have been highlighted many times in the popular press. From a legal viewpoint Spain has not always been the safest place to buy. Most horror stories come at the start of the buying process. It is at the contract and deposit stage where things go wrong, where insufficient checks have been made or inadequate procedures followed.

It cannot be emphasised too strongly that anyone planning to buy a property in Spain must take independent legal advice in a language in which they are fluent from a lawyer experienced in Spanish property law. Always deal with professionals and do not assume that because you may be dealing with a fellow countryman that the advice is better, cheaper or even unbiased.

Do not sign anything, or pay a deposit, until you have sought legal advice. One of the most common phrases heard in Spain is about buyers 'leaving their brains behind at the airport'. It is true! The rush to buy a dream home or a pressurised selling trip or even the euphoria of the moment often make people do incredibly stupid things, literally handing over cash deposits to agents or owners with little or no security.

UNDERSTANDING THE LEGAL DOCUMENTS

Many people choose to buy a new property – not one that is standing empty, completely finished, for these are rare occurrences, but a property that has yet to be built. It may be identical to a show house or built to an individual design to be constructed from a builder's plans. The documentary procedure below should be followed.

- **A plan of the house**. A three-dimensional line drawing, or an architect's plan which shows the dimensions of each floor and each room in square metres.

- **Locating the plot**. A line drawing locating the plot which is called *plan parcial*, a Spanish term meaning a plan of parcels or plots of land.

- **The reservation contract.** This document represents the first step in the buying process. It is an outline agreement to reserve the property.

- **The *nota simple*.** This document, which translated means a 'simple note', is issued by the Land Registry Office and is a copy of the property registration details. It will show proof that the person selling the land or property is the registered owner and there are no debts.

◆ **The purchase contract**. This signifies that the plan of the house and the location of the plot are satisfactory, the *nota simple* has been checked and is in order, and the contract has been read and understood. It releases a non-returnable deposit and signifies the purchaser has the necessary monies to complete the transaction.

◆ **Details of the community charge**. Buying a property in Spain on an urbanisation invariably means becoming a member of a community of property owners. The annual payment and communal facilities should be stated.

◆ **The *certificado final de la dirección de la obra***. Translated this simply means 'certificate of the termination of the building'. It is a certificate produced by the architect when the house is finally complete. It enables a declaration of a new building to be made at the notary's office.

◆ **The *licencia de primera ocupación*** is obtained from the town hall on production of the *cerificado final de la dirección de la obra*. It is a licence to inhabit the property and registers it for the purpose of local taxes and the connection of services.

◆ **Insurance**. A copy of the policy for the property during construction should be available stating the insured value.

◆ **The *escritura*** is the deed for the property. The *copia simple* (not to be confused with the *nota simple*) is a simple copy of the *escritura*, less the signatures, which is sufficient to prove ownership. It is available on the day of signing at the notary and recognised as suitable for most legal purposes. It is normal for the purchaser to hold a copy of this document. The *escritura de compraventa* is the document signed in the notary's office. The *escritura publica* is the *escritura de compraventa* complete with many official stamps from the Property Register, converting it into a public document.

♦ ***Registro de la propiedad.*** This is the last piece of paper in the buying cycle. The *escritura de compraventa* has to be registered with the Property Register making it an *escritura pública* and being over-stamped *registro de la propiedad.* This simple one page document simply closes the loop to the *nota simple* that was considered at the commencement of the buying cycle.

The documentation for a resale property is slightly different:

♦ Obtain a copy of the seller's *escitura.*

♦ Obtain a copy of the *nota simple.*

♦ Obtain a copy of the seller's passport or *residencia.*

♦ Obtain a copy of the seller's *empadronamiento* certificate, which will have been issued by the town hall and which simply states the names of those residing at the address.

♦ Although not always possible, try to obtain a copy of a scale drawing of the property.

♦ If sold furnished, obtain a signed copy of the furniture inventory.

- Obtain the last copy of the paid bills for utilities such as water, electricity and telephone, together with rates and community charges.

- Sign the contract and pay the deposit.

- Sign the *escritura*. Make the final payment. Obtain the *copia simple*.

- Arrange insurances.

- Ensure service and utility supply accounts are changed into the new owner's name.

- Obtain a final copy of the *escritura* and the *registro de la propiedad*.

The first four steps are simply to ensure the person who is selling the house has the right to do so. The name(s) on all the documents should be the same. If not, it is important to find out why. The dimensions of the property in the *escritura* should agree with the dimensions in a scale drawing. If not, this requires investigating as building alteration may have taken place. The seller's *escritura*, the *nota simple* and the financial checks will give details of mortgages and encumbrances on the property. The *copia simple* is the necessary identification required by utility suppliers in order to change the ownership.

MONEY MATTERS

New property
- 10% payment on signing the contract.
- 40% stage payment.
- 25% stage payment.
- 25% on completion.

Resale property
+ 10% on signing the contract.
+ 90% on completion.

A partly built property
+ 50% on signing the contract (walls, roof, windows and doors completed).
+ 25% stage payment.
+ 25% on completion.

The basic rules
+ A deposit of 10% or less is normal for a new or resale property. For a partly built property it will vary according to the amount of work completed. It is payable by cash or banker's draft to the agent or to the seller.

+ The deposit is non-returnable if the buyer fails to complete unless there is a clause in the contract to the contrary.

+ If the builder fails to deliver a new property on time penalty charges accrue. Again these should be stated in the contract. In practice the contract will always state a flexible date of completion.

+ If a seller fails to complete the transaction the buyer is recompensed to a value twice the amount of the deposit unless the contract states otherwise.

+ Final and stage payments should be paid by banker's draft in euros.

Allowing for additional buying costs
It is normal to allow 10% of the property value declared

in the *escritura* for the additional costs in buying which covers three taxes, two fees and charges from the *abogado*. A breakdown of these costs is as follows:

- Transfer tax or IVA (value added tax)   7%
- Stamp duty on a new property only   0.5%
- Plus *valia tax*   0.5%
- Notary Fees   0.5%
- Property Register fees   0.5%
- Charges from the *abogado*   1.0%

Black money

It is quite common in Spain to have two purchase prices for a property.

- One price is the actual price paid exclusive of any fees or taxes.

- The other is a lower price declared in the *escritura*.

- As a guideline, the difference between the two prices should be less than 15 to 20%.

- The difference between the two prices is normally paid to the vendor in cash.

Agents, buyers and sellers, builders and developers, the *abogado,* the bank manager and the notary are aware of what goes on. The tax authorities know it. In fact everyone knows it. It is a mechanism of tax evasion, which if not radically abused, is tolerated by the Spanish tax authorities. Many people are now seeing the folly of this practice but once started it is difficult to stop. The saving on initial taxes when purchasing can easily be outweighed by a greater loss in capital gains when reselling.

SUMMARY

◆ There are many types of property available in Spain. Apartments are the most popular. Linked houses, corner properties, detached properties, traditional houses and *fincas* are others.

◆ Life on an urbanisation or in a community property can be easy.

◆ A property can be by the sea, in the country, new or resale.

◆ Consider the direction it faces. Does it have the magical ingredient of position?

◆ The people involved in the buying process all have a role to play. They are the agent, the *abogado*, the bank manager, the *notario* and the *gestor*.

◆ Allow 10% for legal costs.

◆ There are different legal procedures for different types of property.

◆ Black money is nearly always present in a property transaction.

The Education System

The state-funded school system – co-educational, highly structured, lengthy and free – has been overhauled in the last decade bringing it in line with European educational standards. The state educational system runs alongside private, foreign and international schools. It is compulsory between ages 6 to 16 (see Figure 6). Learning is a serious matter with both students and parents committed to education as a gateway to a good career. The levels are:

- Pre-school education   Voluntary
- Primary education   Compulsory
- Secondary education   Compulsory
- *Bachillerato*   Voluntary
- Vocational training   Voluntary
- University   Voluntary

Pre-school	Voluntary	1 to 6 years	State	Private
Primary	Compulsory	6 to 12 years	State	Private
Secondary	Compulsory	12 to 16 years	State	Private
Bachillerato	Voluntary	16 to 17 years	State	No
Vocational training	Voluntary	16 to 18 years	State	No
University	Voluntary	18 years plus	State	No

Figure 6. Education at a glance

PRE-SCHOOL EDUCATION

Pre-school education is divided into two parts. The first part is for ages 1 to 3 and the second part for ages 4 to 6. Attendance is both voluntary and free with nearly all children aged between 4 and 6 attending for some time before starting primary education. The free state pre-schools are supplemented by private fee-paying nursery schools. Introducing children to the school environment, coordination skills and developing self-awareness and group activities are the objectives of pre-school education.

PRIMARY SCHOOL

Compulsory primary education begins at 6 years of age, for a period of six years, ending at age 12. There are three cycles each of two years during which the student is continuously evaluated. In addition to standard subjects the curriculum includes, where appropriate, an autonomous local language, music, physical education and a foreign language, which is usually English. Students who pass this stage go onto secondary education, but those who do not have to repeat the final year.

SECONDARY SCHOOL

Compulsory secondary education runs from age 12 to 16 years. It completes the compulsory part of education, successful pupils entering *bachillerato* or vocational training. The four years of secondary school are divided into two, two-year cycles, with the curriculum containing both compulsory and optional subjects. The curriculum is not all academic and technical subjects, part of the vocational training, are introduced.

A pupil who does not pass the first cycle is required to repeat a year. Successful students at the end of the second cycle are awarded a 'Graduate in Secondary Education'. Those not successful receive a Certificate stating the school years completed and the qualifications obtained in each subject. About 50% of pupils drop out of the full-time educational system at this point.

BACHILLERATO
Bachillerato unificado y polivalente or BUP simply means 'a pupil who has passed his graduation exam'. It is a non-compulsory part of secondary education providing pupils with two, free, academic courses, each of one year's duration. It is a gateway to the university entrance exam or advanced vocational training and a bridge between school and the mature world outside. In addition to the core subjects four modes exist in the arts, health and environment, technology and social sciences. Some modes are obligatory in order to follow certain university courses. The *bachillerato* is recognised as an entrance qualification by universities worldwide.

VOCATIONAL TRAINING
The first part of free vocational training provides a general introduction to a practical, technical career such as clerical work, electronics, graphics, design or hair-dressing. The second part provides specialised training with pupils dividing their time between studies and on-the-job training.

Given a choice between *bachillerato* and vocational training the trend is towards vocational training. Why?

A job and earnings are close to hand. The thought of a long education through university is daunting. It is also easier for the less academically gifted. However, there is flexibility between educational establishments, the labour market, and vocational training, which enables successful pupils to take additional specialist *bachillerato* courses and then proceed to higher education.

UNIVERSITIES

There are four different types of university establishment:

◆ university schools where a three-year vocational diploma is offered in a subject like teaching or nursing;

◆ university colleges where a three-year course of study leading to a *licenciado* is completed;

◆ faculties where five-year courses are offered in all academic disciplines leading to the equivalent of an MSc and with further studies the equivalent of a PhD;

◆ advanced technical engineering or architecture where five-year technical courses are undertaken.

About a quarter of all pupils go to university. The education standards are comparable with the best in Europe. Foreign universities, where courses are shorter and more flexible, attract wealthy Spanish students.

PRIVATE SCHOOLS

Around a quarter of all Spain's schoolchildren attend private schools. They have smaller classes, are more relaxed and have a less rigid regime than state schools.

XABIA INTERNATIONAL COLLEGE

SETTING STANDARDS FOR ACADEMIC EXCELLENCE IN A NEW EUROPE

With a highly professional, well-qualified team of teachers

PRIMARY DEPARTMENT
Nursery and Reception (3–5)
Learning through free and
structured play in a
stimulating environment.
Infants (5–7)
Introduced to
the English National
Curriculum, Spanish
language and culture.

Juniors (8–11)
Developing skills in a more
formal academic setting.

SECONDARY DEPARTMENT
Wide range of courses leading to
IGCSE and new A/S + A Level
examinations.
Fully equipped Science Labs.
IT centre with Internet and
multi-media facilities.
Large 6th form – over 50 students.
Music, Sport and Drama
Participation in community
events.
Meals provided daily.
Wide-ranging Adults' Studies
programme.

Dining Room with hot meals
daily.
Extensive after-school
curriculum. Highly developed
facilities for Art, Music, Drama
and PE.

Tel: 966472121 e-mail: xicprim@teleline.es.
Tel: 966471785 e-mail: xic@ctv.es
Bus Service from Altea and Denia
Membership of ECIS and NABSS
Exam Centre for Cambridge and London Boards

Figure 7. Spanish education, English style

This wide range of private, co-educational schooling embraces Spanish, bilingual and international schools following a variety of syllabi including the British and Spanish examination systems (see Figure 7). However, most Spanish private schools teach wholly in Spanish, are state-subsidised and follow the Spanish state-school curriculum. Some international schools follow the Spanish curriculum but bilingually in English and Spanish. This provides language skills to the pupils and attracts a state subsidy.

English-speaking parents with young children will be aware that the sooner a child is exposed to a multilingual situation the better. Conversely an older child will find more problems adjusting. Foreign parents often prefer to educate younger children in Spanish nursery and primary schools, where they quickly learn Spanish, and then send children of secondary school age to a private school.

The British Council, mentioned earlier, has details of many English-speaking schools.

DID YOU KNOW?
Social structure

It may be surprising to know that Spain has a complex social structure. It is another legacy from the past. Let's look at some of the levels:

- The Royal family – top of the pile

- Grandees – the leading nobility having a gateway to all the correct social circles

+ Nobles – with an assortment of various titles

+ Politicians – suitably despised

+ Professional – working directors or business owners

+ White-collar workers and blue-collar workers

+ New resident foreigners – wealthier than gypsies and Moroccans

+ Gypsies – near the bottom of the pile except when fighting bulls or flamenco dancing

+ Moroccans – at the bottom of the pile

The education system and cultural differences, intentionally or unintentionally, preserve this social structure.

SUMMARY

+ Education in Spain is compatible with European standards, but lengthy.

+ There is a strong emphasis on pre-school education, *bachillerato* and vocational training.

+ Many private schools exist, some English-speaking.

+ For a young child it is important to get immersed in the Spanish language as quickly as possible.

+ Spain's universities are excellent.

+ A social class structure exists.

9

Culture

THE ROMANTIC CULTURE OF OLD SPAIN

Flamenco

The popular, romantic image of Spain, namely flamenco, singing and dancing gypsies, together with swaggering bullfighters is unreal. But flamenco does occupy an important place in Spanish culture, particularly in Andalucian culture. It is not simply preserved folklore, but rather a vibrant and important art of song and dance. It is certainly true that a version of flamenco has been commercialised and turned into a sanitised spectacle. This sometimes bears little relation to the raw vigour of the real thing.

The problem for the spectator is where to see and hear the real thing. To find *cante jondo* (deep song), which is the authentic, heart-rending sound of flamenco, or its other pure forms there is a need to enquire if there is a *peña flamenca* (a flamenco club) or *un bar donde se canta flamenco* (a bar where flamenco is sung). A more commercial *tablao flamenco* (flamenco show) is available in many of the larger Andalucian cities such as Seville, Córdoba, Granada and coastal tourist resorts.

In the south during the late spring and summer it is possible to discover local *ferias* (festivals) where it is possible to experience a version of flamenco song and dance called the *sevillana*. Even in the smallest villages groups of people can be found, many in costume, singing and clapping to the rhythm, while the dancers wind themselves around each other in what can only be described as a controlled and highly stylised dance.

Fiestas

Fiestas celebrate a national religious occasion or a local thanksgiving where towns and cities come to a stop as men, women and children dress up to enjoy themselves aided by a plentiful supply of food, wine and laughter. Processions with music start the evening, dancing and singing follow. Fireworks close the evening with a loud colourful bang. Each fiesta has its own distinctive character – sounds, colours, flavours, smells, costumes, rituals and a typical dish. There are celebrations for the dead and the living. Some fiestas appease the forces of nature. Others drive out evil spirits. Often they are based on historical events or include medieval or ancient customs. There is always a fiesta somewhere. They can last for a day, a week or a fortnight.

Perhaps the best-known fiesta is the one in celebration of the reconquest of the Moors by the Christians held at Alcoy near Alicante but also replicated in many other Spanish towns in that region. Throughout the world there are many colourful processions but few can compare with the medieval pageantry which is accompanied by the music of brass instruments and loud kettle drums, as the marchers slowly sway rhythmically in the early darkness of a summer's evening.

EL TORO (THE BULL)

Bullfighting

This is not the place to discuss the morality of a bullfight but it is worth making one important point. Most foreigners are aware that in the bullfight several bulls are going to be injured in various ways. They will be lanced, they will have sharp barbs stuck in them and in the end they will be killed, more or less efficiently, with a sword. There will be blood and there will be death. If a foreigner does not want to see this, or may be upset by it, or if they think it is barbaric and cruel, then it is really not worth going because they will certainly not enjoy it.

Posters

Bullfights are always advertised on posters in bars or on the street. The posters will announce whether it is to be a *corrida de toros* – a bullfight with four- to six-year-old bulls and with senior *matadores* or a *corrida de novillos* – with younger bulls and junior *matadores*. Additional information given on the poster will include the name of the ranch supplying the bulls and the names of the *matadores* who will be listed in order of seniority and performance. The posters will give the place, date and time of the bullfight. The bullring is called *la plaza de toros*.

Seating

The major distinction between the seats at a bullfight is between those in the *sol* (sun) and those in the *sombra* (shade). There are also tickets called *sol y sombra* (sun and shade), which are for seats that start in the sun but are in the shade by the middle of the event. *Sol* tickets are much cheaper than *sombra* and most of the activity takes place on the *sombra* side of the arena. As you go in people will probably be renting cushions. Since the seats will be stone, brick or concrete, it is a good investment.

The format

Six bulls are fought in a normal bullfight. They are not domestic animals that have been maltreated to make them aggressive. They are a breed of bull raised on specialist ranches. In a herd in the field they are tranquil but once isolated and in a closed space they are fearsome. They are fast, deadly accurate with their horns and have so much strength that they can lift a man as though he were a rag doll.

Three teams perform during the afternoon. Each of them consists of:

◆ a *matador*, who is the main performer and will kill two of the bulls;

◆ three *banderilleros*, his foot assistants who help him with their cape work and who also stick the *banderillas* (coloured sticks) into the bulls;

◆ two *picadores*, who are mounted on heavily padded horses and armed with a metal-tipped lance which they use to stab the bull.

The *matadores* perform in order of seniority determined by the date on which they were registered and not in order of fame or popularity. The senior man will take the first and fourth, the next most senior the second and fifth, and the last the third and sixth.

The entry of the bull

When the arena is clear the president will signal with the use of a white handkerchief for the first bull to be released; trumpets sound and the door to the bull pen is opened. Above the door is a number; this is the weight of the bull. A good bull will charge into the arena and attack anything that moves. It is not a good sign if a bull looks back towards the pens or is unwilling to come out. Contrary to the popular image, a bull which paws the ground before attacking is not particularly ferocious; it is in fact slightly cowardly because it is threatening without wanting to charge.

The first passes

The *matador*, or more usually one of his assistants, will make a few passes with the large, pink-and-yellow cape to try to work out the quality of the bull. The *matador* needs to know whether it will charge, whether it can see properly, and whether it attacks better with its left or right horn. After a few passes the president will signal for the next act to begin. When the matador takes over is he calm and still? Ideally he should have his hands held low and move the cape slowly and gracefully. He should be able to slow down the bull's charge in this way. He should step into the bull's path and at the moment the bull reaches him he should be still. A step backwards is not a good sign. The correct impression is that he is the one in control.

The *picador*

The *picador* on a well-padded horse is led into the arena and the bull is encouraged to the opposite side. Once the first *picador* is in position, which usually takes place on the shady side, the *matador* or one of his assistants goads the bull into charging the horse. The *picador* then plunges the metal-spiked tip of his lance into the large hump on the bull's shoulders. The bull receives two lance thrusts, the object being to reduce the strength of the bull, and to break down the strong neck muscles so that the bull charges with its head down thus allowing the *matador* to work closer.

The *banderilleros*

Once again the president signals for the act to be changed. The trumpets sound and the *picadores* leave the arena. The *matadores* who are not performing come into the arena to help the *banderilleros*. Two of the three *banderilleros* perform at this point. The first holds a *banderilla* in each hand and, once he has the bull's attention, runs in a curving path towards the bull, which is itself running towards him. When they meet he thrusts the *banderillas* into the hump on the neck of the bull and turns around its flank to escape. The second *banderillero* repeats the process. The careful placing of the *banderillas* can alter the way a bull charges.

The *banderilleros* are judged by elegance of movement and control. At the moment of placing the *banderillas* the man should ideally have his feet together with both off the ground. The *banderillas* should be placed close together in the hump. As he turns away from the bull, he only needs to run a few steps and then walk away calmly to indicate he is well in control and the bull is being truly dominated.

The final stage

Once the *banderilleros* have finished their work the final

act begins. With his first bull of the afternoon the *matador* will take his sword, the *muleta*, a small, red, cape-like cloth and approach the presidential box. He will salute the president with hat in hand and formally ask permission to perform and kill the bull.

The *matador* has a whole repertoire to select from for this part of his performance, which will last about ten minutes. When he judges that it is time to kill the bull he uses his *muleta* to encourage the bull to charge and when the two are almost in contact, leans over the horns and thrusts the sword in between its shoulder blades.

Even with a good sword thrust the bull will not necessarily die immediately, but the audience will still applaud, because they are interested in seeing the man risk himself. This is the moment of truth. If a bullfighter has performed badly then he will be greeted with either silence or jeers, abuse and whistles. If he has been reasonably good he will be applauded and will step into the arena to acknowledge this. Should the applause continue he and his *banderilleros* will take a lap of honour.

On some occasions *matadores* are caught by bulls and badly gored. Some foreigners stand and loudly applaud the bull. But this is one piece of visitor behaviour that does upset Spaniards. It provokes a horrified and indignant response, as they are unable to understand how the suffering and possible death of a human being could be greeted with such applause. But they do recognise it happens. One of the most famous Spanish poems is an elegy, written by Lorca, a lament for the bullfighter Ignacio Sanchez Mejias who was gored to death at five in the afternoon.

> At five in the afternoon
> It was five in the afternoon exactly
> A child brought the white sheet
> At five in the afternoon
> The rest was death and death only
> At five in the afternoon
> A coffin on wheels was his bed
> At five in the afternoon
> Bones and flutes echo in his ear
> At five in the afternoon
> How terrible this five in the afternoon.

Bull running

The world-famous event involving fighting bulls is of course the Pamplona Bull Run. There are many other fiestas in Spanish towns and villages where young and frisky, lean and mean fighting bulls are turned loose in closed-off central squares. Bulls are not injured in these events but the only real defence against them are good strong legs.

It is important to stress that there is nothing fake about these events. The bulls are real and extremely dangerous, and people, even experienced runners, have been badly injured or killed. If you enjoy raw excitement and the thrill of adrenalin pumping through your system then you will certainly find it running the bulls.

THE SPANISH CHARACTER

What is the Spanish character?

.What makes a Spaniard a Spaniard? The Basques are different in some ways from Castilians, who are different from Catalans, who are different from Andalucians, who are different from Galicians, and so on... However, it is possible to construct a general image of Spaniards, as distinct from the French, the Americans or the British (see Figure 8).

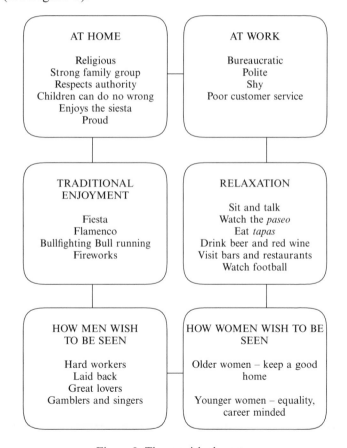

Figure 8. The spanish character

Pride

Familiarity is a hallmark of Spanish life. Handshaking and kissing on the cheek is the usual form of greeting. Old-fashioned courtliness and formal manners are, however, still a custom in rural areas. Great store is set by personal loyalty and friendship, but it is also very important to take account of a Spaniard's personal sense of honour and pride, which is easily offended. Initially an advertising logo and how a national sense of pride, is symbolised by the black bull. It can be seen everywhere, as a gigantic shape next to a road or as a car sticker (see Figure 9).

Figure 9. The black bull

Conversation

One important character to be relied upon is the Spaniard's readiness to communicate. Compare the discreet silence of a group of English people who do not know each other to the friendly chatter which quickly develops among a similar group of Spanish people. A good deal of social life is maintained *en la calle* (in the street) or any public place. Bars are particularly important. Spaniards generally enjoy conversation, invariably loud, where everyone seems to talk at once and the excited babble of noise has the ability to penetrate both bricks and mortar.

The language barrier

A foreigner, away from the areas of mass tourism, may well be stared at as an object of curiosity, but it is easy to turn this round by attempting to overcome the language barrier by starting a simple conversation with odd phrases and expressive gestures. Spaniards are generally pleased when a foreigner makes an effort to speak their language. They are remarkably patient with someone who is trying to communicate and they listen carefully in an attempt to make sense of the mangled grammar and odd vocabulary. Exactly 'how' it is said it is less important than 'wanting' to say it.

Religion

Catholicism is still an influence over Spanish society. Although church attendance is falling, on a Sunday, around midday, families can be seen dressed in their best attire strolling home from their place of worship. The images of saints watch over shops, bars and drivers' cabs. Traditional fiestas mark church feasts. However, during the Civil War the Church aligned itself with Franco and some people have never forgiven it for this.

Politeness

Anyone who has spent a short time in Spain will know that its people are friendly. If you are polite, smile, and offer locals a greeting in their own language it will go a long way to establishing and maintaining relationships.

However, it would be fair to say in tourist resorts a perceived need to extract the maximum euros in the minimum time has eroded some of the natural charm of the Spaniard. A few Spaniards too find it difficult to handle their newfound wealth. But it would be wrong to categorise the whole country for the behaviour patterns of a few.

As one might expect, there is a contrast between the older and younger generations. The more elderly Spaniard will have endured the repression of the Franco years, may be illiterate and have worked in agriculture. In contrast his offspring will be vibrant, computer literate and with a city-based mentality that embraces new cosmopolitan values.

The family group

The family group is strong with sometimes two or three generations living within one house. The Spanish love of children is well known. Children will be beautifully dressed with a confidence that befits offspring in the new millennium. Mother and father will be proud parents with a deep sense of honour. Grandparents will be friendly, courteous, generous, not fully comprehending the staggering changes that have taken place since their childhood.

The young handsome male will study in the evening for personal advancement, will watch football and own a fast scooter. The beautiful dark haired *senorita* will be of slim build and somehow be one foot taller and one foot narrower than her mother. Young Spaniards are the same as the young of any European country, seeking freedom, equality and enjoyment alongside their worldly brothers and sisters.

The *paseo*

Outside the restaurant, in the main square or along the promenade the evening *paseo* will commence with young girls and boys, parents and grandparents strolling in a leisurely manner. For some it is gentle exercise in the cool of the evening, for others a prelude to a good night out; for the spectators, it is an entertainment.

In villages chairs are placed in the narrow streets, oblivious to passing traffic, as occupants emerge from their houses, to talk and gossip about the day's events.

How not to be an Inglés

'Inglés' is a word sometimes used disparagingly about tourists or foreigners living in rural Spain. It is about their colour, their dress and humour. Alternatively, it is not doing things that the Spanish do! So how do you avoid being treated as Inglés? The answer is actually quite simple. Be sensitive to Spanish codes of behaviour.

The first characteristic is the way a person's white skin is burned to a colour resembling freshly cooked salmon. Not for the Inglés a light tan or weatherbeaten complexion but one that demonstrates to all and sundry a skin little exposed to the sunlight.

Shorts and beachwear are not an appropriate dress for urban areas, whether this is city, town or village. It is not that Spaniards are particularly prudish about the sight of bare flesh, for they too will wear skimpy bikinis and shorts on the beach. The concern is where the flesh is revealed.

Humour can differ too.

Sebastian, a new resident foreigner, was cutting some leaves off his palm tree. Paco, complete with donkey and cart, passes by.

Sebastian rushes out with a bucket and spade. He picks up the donkey droppings.

Paco asks, '¿Que senor, que?' (Why?).

'To put on my rhubarb,' says Sebastian.

'Señor, in Spain we put custard on our rhubarb. Are you an Inglés?'

Getting things done

Spanish bureaucrats, in common with those of other nations, when asked to render a service often find it easier to say 'no' than to say 'yes'. Spaniards are in general insistent in their demands, whether this be in a market, a bar or government office. They most certainly do not easily accept 'no' for an answer, and new residents should not either.

When something really needs to be done that is being refused, it is best to remain patient but persistent. Losing your temper or becoming angry in such circumstances is counterproductive. The trick is to maintain a conversation, keep the bureaucrat's attention and get him to respond to you as a person and not simply a problem.

So much in Spain is achieved through a network of individual contacts and friends of friends that many problems can be resolved through these channels. It is not always possible to buy your way out of problems or difficulties, but things do get done for friends.

The *siesta*

Big cities mean that people cannot get from work to home and back again in the lunchbreak, and a change in working hours similar to northern Europe is reducing the importance of the *siesta*. In some parts of Spain it is still a common practice and it is best to expect very little activity between 1.30 pm and about 4.30 pm, when offices, public buildings and shops tend to be closed. The *siesta* is, however, particularly significant during the summer when many parts of Spain are blisteringly hot and the only sensible thing to do is to rest behind closed shutters. A *siesta* also allows the body to deal with late Spanish nightlife.

DID YOU KNOW?
Customs

Fire and fireworks

Light, fire, gunpowder are key elements in fiestas. *Las fallas* are unparalleled fiestas of fire signifying renovation, spring-cleaning and a change in season. Huge caricatures of politicians, film stars and comic-strip personalities, full of satire and humour, are erected in the streets, and then, to the accompaniment of a firework display, at midnight they are set on fire. The following day plans are made for next year's figures.

But the following statement encapsulates a problem.

The council has issued a new by-law banning unlicensed firework displays and imposing strict guidelines which private companies must adhere to in order to safeguard the public. The new by-law was pushed through after last year's fiesta season saw deaths and serious injuries caused by lax regulations.

Children are brought up to the noise of fireworks and crackers. Factories make them. Shops import 'bangers' from China. Pocket money is spent on making a noise irrespective of the time, place or occasion. Pets huddle in corners, frightened. The tolerant adult Spaniard just smiles. After all they are children, they can do no wrong.

Toilets

Try to find a public toilet in Spain – it's easier to find a needle in a haystack. Except in railway stations, shopping centres and places of public interest they don't exist. What do you do? Answer, go to a bar, café, hotel or restaurant nearby. Owners of food establishments are well accustomed to this behaviour, granting a request to use their facilities with a smile or a wave of the hand. Here are a few essential words:

> *Damas* = ladies   *Caballeros* = men
> *Senoras* = women   *Senores* = men
> *Tiolet* = servicios or, aseos
> Where is the toilet? = *¿Donde estan los servicios por favor?*
> Are there toilets here? = *¿Hay servicios por favor?*

Gambling and the lottery

Like the people of all the Mediterranean countries, the Spaniard loves to gamble. It is, however, focused on the state national lottery (*Lotería Nacional*) run in aid of charities where tickets can be purchased at offices, from street vendors and through the Society for the Blind (ONCE).

The world's biggest lottery takes place each Christmas (*El Gordo*). Ticket prices are high and therefore mainly sold to syndicates with the winners arguing over the spoils. *El Niño* (The Kid), the second biggest lottery, takes place in early January.

In addition many regulated casinos in resort areas, with well dressed, well heeled clientele, play roulette, blackjack and *chemin de fer*, offering yet another more sophisticated method of losing money.

Nightclubs

Along busy main roads or in cities, flashing neon lights beckon the unwary into a nightclub. These are not cabaret, musical or dancing extravaganzas. If not eating, drinking red wine or singing the Spanish male has a reputation of being a great lover. That may, or may not be the case, and for all we know a nightclub may be the place to learn for they are registered or unregistered brothels. It is certainly not a place to take your mother or sister.

Chufa

So you think all Spaniards drink red wine, sherry and cognac with the occasional strong light beer at weekends? Well they do, and that's the image macho drinking males wish to preserve. Deep down they have a distinct partiality to Chufa. What is that you may well ask?

It's similar in Scotland where the national drink is Irn Bru and not, contrary to popular opinion, whisky. Chufa is a non-alcoholic drink, unique to Spain, being the diluted juices of the sedge root plant called *chufa*. Like so many things, the Moors introduced it to Spain. It is in Valencia that Horchata (another name for Chufa) is most popular and it can be drunk in *horchaterias*, served with cakes and pastries. It can also be bought in bottles from supermarkets. It is marketed similar to sterilised milk and in summer is sold in ice cream shops as an alternative to a branded, chilled soft drink. If you're feeling sluggish, Horchata is good for an energy boost.

SUMMARY

◆ The romantic culture of old Spain embraces flamenco and fiestas. These activities still occur today but often in a sanitised, commercial way.

◆ Fighting *el toro* and bull running are very popular. Bullfighting can be viewed as a cruel, bloody sport, or a heroic, artistic spectacle.

◆ It is difficult to define the Spanish character. It is a way of life.

◆ The Spaniard tends to be polite, verbose, part of a strong family group, religious and proud.

◆ They relax in the cool of the evening by watching, talking and eating.

◆ The siesta is decreasing in importance, but in the hot summer, is still a necessity.

- Spanish bureaucrats are plentiful. Deal with them by being persistent.

- It is necessary to understand some customs, how they arise and how to deal with them.

- Fireworks in the correct place are fine, but often are a nuisance.

- Remember there are few public toilets.

(10)

Savouring Food and Wine

THE PLEASURE OF GOOD FOOD

In recent years Spanish food and restaurateurs have made great strides forward. In the most unimaginable places, sometimes hidden away in villages of the interior or next door to a tourist resort along the coast one can find restaurants with a style of their own, offering quality products, practising modern Mediterranean cuisine and sometimes delving into the avant-garde, but always faithful to their roots, making extraordinarily healthy dishes.

CLASSIC DISHES OF SPAIN

Gazpacho

Gazpacho is a chilled raw soup originating in Andalucia that is made by pounding bread and garlic with tomatoes, cucumber and peppers. Olive oil and vinegar gives it a refreshing tang. It is usually garnished with diced salad vegetables and croutons.

Paella

Is this the national dish of Spain? Consisting mainly of rice seasoned with saffron, it can be a combination of chicken, vegetables and seafood, or a combination of sausages, rabbit and meat with chickpeas. Each region will have its own variation. Although many people consider paella the most typical of Spanish dishes, its origins are fairly recent. The first paella was prepared in Valencia in the late nineteenth century.

It is cooked in a flat metal pan with two handles riveted to the sides. Paella short grain rice can be prepared with chicken or rabbit or both, with shellfish, fish of various kinds, or with vegetables only. The combinations are practically limitless – ranging from meatless 'Lent' paella containing only salted codfish and cauliflower, to paella made using small game fresh from the hunt.

It is a popular dish at fiesta time, and curiously enough, a masculine meal customarily made by men. The Valencian phrase 'to go paella-eating' is used throughout the region, which may involve outings, parties, picnics and such like.

The genuine Valencian paella always has a good helping of wide-pod green beans and giant dried butter beans. As for meats, chicken, pork and rabbit are used and occasionally wild duck. Adding extra flavour are white-shelled mountain snails providing what some call an exquisite taste. But there are also seafood and shellfish paellas, which in recent years have become increasingly popular, particularly the high-priced mouth-watering lobster paella.

Whatever the ingredients may be, when an orthodox paella reaches the table, the grains of rice should be dry, loose and golden, never mushy or sticky or leaving a trace of oil if served on the plate. When the paella has been cooked over an outdoor wood fire, the paella-eating ritual calls for diners to sit in a circle, to eat from the communal pan and to scrape the nearly burnt rice from the bottom. Some say this is the best part.

Cocido

Many people consider the traditional meal of Spain to be a meat stew called *cocido*. It is a slow-simmered stew of beef, chicken, ham and pork belly with chickpeas, cabbage, *chorizo* (red sausage) and *morcilla* (black sausage) producing a dish usually served in three courses. The broth is served first, then the vegetables and then the meats.

In Madrid it is called *cocido a la madrileña*. It is a stew of chicken, *chorizo* sausage, maybe some ham or other cured meat, potatoes, cabbage and chickpeas and macaroni. Again it is eaten 'from front to back'. But this is a dull dish. There are so many good things to eat in Spain why bother with *cocido*. Yet the people of Madrid love, dream and sing about it.

Sweets of Moorish origin

Sweet floury breads halfway between normal bread and confectionery are zealously eaten together with pastries and confectionery. To this list should be added *leche merengada* (ice cream made from milk, egg whites and flavourings) and crisp almond cookies called *avellana*. Top of the list for sweet-toothed performers in Spanish gastronomy is none other than the nougat-like *turrones* from Xixona made from the abundance of almonds and honey produced in various districts of the province.

EATING WELL

Cutting the ham

In town and country no bar or supermarket will be without festoons of *jamón* hanging from the ceiling. It seems an unnatural thing to do, hanging fresh meat in a warm place with lots of people around and in some cases lots of tobacco smoke too. But it tastes good.

The English words 'ham and gammon' and the Spanish words *jamón york* all mean much the same thing. The leg joint of the pig is processed with water, salt and preservatives. Parma ham and the Spanish variety, *jamón serrano*, is simply hung and cured on the bone for a long period of time in carefully controlled conditions of temperature and humidity.

Mountain ham from white pigs fed on acorns gives almost the best Serrano but the premier product is the *pata negra* from Huelva, which is produced from brown pigs with black feet and cured for 12 to 18 months. How do you get the wafer thin slices of tender ham? The leg is clamped into a wooden rack while a long sharp knife shaves the thin strips.

The bigger cities have places that specialise in offering ham for sale. Customers will be stand around the bar eating plates of ham cut off the bone, *manchego* cheese, crusty bread with loads of olives and drinking glasses of red wine. Some say it is the food of the gods!

Slicing the sausage

Dry, long-life, colourful, sausages in different shapes and

sizes hang in the supermarket next to hams. To understand sausages let us consider their general types: the raw and the smoked. Under raw we have the red, black and white. Under the smoked we have the black and the white.

Chorizo is the most common cured, red sausage. The colouring is achieved by paprika, the dried powder of the ground sweet red capsicum. This along with salt, garlic and black pepper is used to season a ground mixture of pork and pork fat. It is smoked or hung to dry like ham. It has a bright red colour, a chewy texture and a spicy taste.

Salchichon and *longaniza* are cured white sausages. They are similar to chorizo but made without paprika. Some variations are spiced with oregano or nutmeg. Others are more delicate. They are round and can be very long and thin.

Morcilla is a cooked Spanish black pudding. In the *morcilla* recipe are blood, pork fat, salt and spices, onion or chopped nuts. A very common addition is cooked rice. Some *morcillas* are sweet. Its soft texture does not need chewing.

Lastly are the white cooked sausages called *butifarras*. Like *morcillas*, they are made right after slaughter and cooked with spices and other ingredients. They are the least popular of the Spanish sausages.

Food from the sea
The Spanish have always ventured seaward in search of food, adventure and trade. While each region has its

traditional specialties, there is hardly a fish you cannot find in any major city. Like the Italians the Spanish will eat any creature that emerges from the depths. When it comes to fish their favorites are *bonito* (tuna), *bacala* (cod), *sardinas* (sardines), *anchoas* (anchovies) and *pulpo* (octopus). As for shellfish *gambas* (prawns) has to be one of the favourites.

Lovers of fish will drool at the sight of masses of different fish species on offer in supermarkets, although some sizes are ridiculously small and should never have been caught. But it not the intention to knock the Spanish fishing fleets as you should also see some of the big crabs! Some of the other typical fish from which delicious dishes are made include, hake, red mullet, sole, swordfish, gray mullet, narrow-mouthed cat shark, cuttlefish, redfish, mackerel, blue-mouth rockfish, wreck-fish and rays. Fantastic salmon is imported from Norway.

Wisdom is often to be found in simplicity. Fish and shellfish in Spain are usually prepared in uncomplicated yet mouth-watering ways: baked in the oven, hot from the grill, done over charcoal, lightly fried or cooked in succulent yet simple stews.

Cheeses
Although the range of Spanish cheeses is impressive they cannot be compared with the variety available in either France or the UK. A good *manchego* cheese will have been made under government regulation giving a consistent and reliable product. The hard sheep's milk cheeses from the heart of Spain's La Mancha are

delightful when well matured. *Cabrales*, a sheep's cheese rather like Roquefort, is also worth trying.

Fruit and vegetables

Spain is the market garden of Europe having almost every climate and microclimate. It produces and exports more fruit and vegetables than most other nations of the EU. The range of fruit and vegetables available to the Spanish cook is enviable.

Strangely Spanish fresh fruit and vegetables have to be purchased with care. Locally grown produce in season is cheap and available all year long, but of course like all European countries Spain exports most of its Class I produce. Quality produce is better purchased from the *fruteria* at the *mercado central* than from the supermarket.

REGIONAL FOOD

Green Spain

Some of the most delicious seafood comes from the Atlantic coast with specialities including mussels, scallops, lobsters and octopus. The north coast also supplies crabs, anchovies and tuna. Soft and blue cheese comes from the mountains of Cantabria. Later in this chapter it will be seen that it is wine that gives this region its fame. Spain's most prestigious red wine, Rioja, is matured to a distinctive vanilla mellowness as the grape is influenced during its growth on hilly stony soil by both the Mediterranean and Atlantic weather systems.

Eastern Spain

Catalina too is known for good food. *Amanida* is a salad with vegetables, cured meat, cheese and fish, *Sequet* a fish and shellfish stew. Sausages come in all shapes, sizes and colours. But the most famous dish is a pudding called *crema Catalán* – a rich egg custard with a golden brown layer of grilled sugar on top, served very cold.

Andalucia

Its historic Arab inhabitants have heavily influenced the food of this area. Traditionally almonds, rice, lemons, oranges, grapes and olives were grown. Today's crops now include strawberries, apples, melons, cherries and pears. Barbecued meats, sauces flavoured with cumin or saffron, sweets made from crushed almonds are all typical dishes of today. Grilled fish, especially sardines and *calamares* (squid), and whole fish baked in a crust of salt, are popular dishes.

Central Spain

Game such as wild boar, pheasant and partridge is plentiful in Central Spain. La Mancha maintains a tradition of robust cooking with a variety of one-pot pulse stews. Castilla y León is known for its suckling pig and milk-fed lamb roasted whole in enormous bread ovens. Many convents and shops in Toledo continue to sell popular little marzipan cakes.

The region is of course well known for *cocido* and *patatas a la importancia* that are egg coated potatoes fried and then simmered in wine and *manchego* cheese.

The Islands

Regional food is gradually being squeezed out, but traditional egg dishes still remain to be eaten in good Mallorcan restaurants. In the Canary Islands, however, regional food does not exist, forgotten in the commercial need to provide international blandness. Bananas are grown here, a small, sweet variety often used in fritters and tarts.

DID YOU KNOW?
Anguilas (eels)

The life of the *anguila* (eel) is just as astonishing as the life of the salmon but in reverse. The adult lives in the river then goes to the ocean to spawn and die. When spawning time arrives, they descend the northern Spanish rivers in great shoals, heading out to the Atlantic Ocean and to the Sargasso Sea on the edge of the Bermudas.

They spawn and the females die, leaving their fertilised eggs behind. When they hatch, the elvers are no bigger than a few inches. They begin the long journey home to the rivers of northern Spain. It is an arduous journey. Those that do survive and escape the fishermen's nets will reach up to a metre in length. However, millions are scooped up into gossamer nets, parboiled, put into vacuum packed bags and frozen or rushed off to restaurants where diners allegedly enjoy the catch.

EATING OUT

Food is important. Spaniards enjoy café life. Like the French they live to eat.

Breakfast is a coffee with bread or a croissant. There are three types of coffee. Café *solo* is a small cup of strong coffee not for the thirsty. Café *con leche* is coffee with milk. Café *americano* is a large cup without milk. *Churos* – a doughnut-type fried pastry with hot chocolate – forms a traditional breakfast of mega calories.

Lunch takes place between 2.00 pm and 4.00 pm and if taken outside the home will consist of *tapas* or, alternatively, a light three-course meal with wine and bread.

Dinner is late – starting from 9.00 pm. The Spanish are famous for eating at, what to some, is a ludicrously late hour. Who in most countries would think of sitting down to a full meal at nine o'clock in the evening? This late night eating is all to do with the Spanish siesta-adjusted body clock with most people not finishing work until half past seven or eight o'clock. It is usually a reversal of lunch, but either way with a bit more wine and a bit less food. No one wants to go to bed on a full stomach.

Restaurant meals usually consist of three courses. The choices for *menu del día* are chalked up on a blackboard outside the restaurant. Many restaurants in Spain (including strangely Chinese) offer a meal known as the *menu del día*. It must consist of three courses plus bread, and water or wine. The third course is always dessert. The price is always less than if you were to order the same items à la carte. It is one of the best deals in Spain. There may be only two or three choices per course or as many as a dozen.

With a bottle of table wine and fine food at prices that do not compare with those for a meal in northern Europe (see the prices on the menu of an upmarket golf club shown in Figure 10), eating out can cost next to nothing. It is a constant source of amazement that restaurants can produce a three-course meal with wine for as little as €10. A service charge is included in some restaurant and hotel bills, but waiters will appreciate an additional 5 to 10% tip.

But beware! Among the basic intake of food and drink should be included tobacco. Men smoke, women smoke and teenagers smoke. Wherever you go you will soon be enveloped in a thick blue haze of cigarette smoke and the Spanish seem not to have the faintest idea that this could be uncomfortable to anyone.

TAPAS

In addition to restaurants, there are many attractive *tapas* bars offering freshly made snacks and appetisers. The *tapas* bar is unique to Spain. Alicante is known as one of the best *tapas* areas where the ritual of *tapa* eating has reached sublime levels.

Tapas come in all sorts of delicious forms and are readily available in most bars. Rows of dishes are arranged in a chilled cabinet in front of the customer. They comprise tortilla, spicy meat balls, big plump olives, sausages, fried aubergines, egg salad, courgettes, spicy potatoes, liver, cheese, serrano ham, sardines, prawns in garlic, anchovies, mussels, fried squid, calamares, sepia and small fish in olive oil.

Nibbling at small amounts of food is popular, but of equal importance is the *tapas* bar an essential part of life,

OLIVA NOVA GOLF

ENSALADAS
Preparesela usted mismo a su gusto desde nuestro
buffet de ensaladas compuestas y simples.
Buffet de Ensaladas 5.25€

SANDWICHES Y
BOCADILLOS
Tortilla al gusto 3.25€
Tortilla Española 3.25€
Jamon a la catalán 4.50€
Lomo con queso 4.50€
Pepito de ternera 5.10€
Sepia con all i oli 4.65€
Atun con tomate 3.70€
Sandwich mixto 3.25€
Sandwich vegetal 3.85€
Club sandwich 6.00€
Pan 0.90€
Tostadas 1.50€
Alioli 1.20€

ZAPATAS
Anchoas con tomate y aceitunas 4.75€
Sobrasada y queso 4.75€
Jamón iberico 7.25€

TAPAS Y
MONTADITOS
Tapas del día 3.25€
Montaditos variados del día 1.25€
Jamón serrano 4.25€
Queso manchego 3.30€

Figure 10. Sevy's supper – a menu from the restaurant at the
upmarket Oliva Nova Golf Club. The course was
designed by Ballesteros.

Croquetas de jamón	1.60€
Croquetas de pollo	1.60€
Croquetas de bacalao	1.90€
Gambas al ajillo	8.80€
Calamares a la romana	3.35€
Boquerones en vinagre	3.25€
Pimientos del piquillo	2.25€
Chopitos fritos andaluza	3.30€
Salazones de la terreta	4.90€
Dátiles con bacón	3.10€

PLATOS
COMBINADOS

Escalope Milanesa con patas y esalada	10.20€
Entrecote a la pimienta	12.60€
Costillar de cerdo asado en salsa de naranja	11.00€
Lomo de cerdo con huevo frio y patas	9.00€
Salchichas caseras atomatadas	6.00€
Hamburguesa de terna parrilla	6.00€
Sepia a la parrilla acompanada de pasta	11.00€
Rape en salsa verde	12.00€

ARROCES

Arroz a banda	7.95€
Arroz cadoso de carne o pescado	7.95€
Fideua gandiense	7.95€
Paella valenciana	7.95€
Paella mixa	10.00€

POSTRES

Tartas, pastels y otros	3.50€
Fruira fresca de temporada	3.50€
Helado various	2.50€
Crema Catalan	2.50€

a place where people meet to eat and drink, to gossip, to carry out business and generally to pass the time of day.

BAR OR CAFÉ

A bar is mainly a male-dominated environment serving beer, wine and *tapas*. They may specialise, creating an individual image through music, cocktails, cabaret or beer. Picture a popular bar situated in a tiny street of a small village about 10 a. m., a scene that is enacted throughout the whole of Spain – dark, with basic tables and chairs, walls painted some time ago in a murky yellow colour or any colour provided it is murky. A stuffed boar's head adorns the wall; the shelves contain a variety of silver cups for football behind which are pictures of the teams. There is also a large picture of grandfather looking starched and bemused, a proud man holding a horse, of grandmother starched and not amused, of pretty granddaughters and daughters in their national costumes taken during one of the many fiestas. Also dotted around are gaming machines, dart boards, posters displaying ice creams, boxes of crisps, wines, beer and spirits. That's just the wall.

All along the base of the bar, especially first thing in the morning, are cigarette ends. They do get brushed up but are soon replaced as the older Spaniard doesn't bother with an ashtray. The top of the bar will be littered with plates, cups and saucers, glasses, bottles and the remains of food.

The noise of people talking will be deafening as they all talk at the same time. Later on in the morning, when everything has been brushed up and the bar surface cleared, the older retired men will take up positions at the tables and either play cards or dominoes. Bars in villages and towns are social clubs where people meet and keep abreast of what is happening aided by watching the inevitable television set high up in a corner that can be showing anything from football to bullfighting to naked bodies doing 'unmentionables'. As it is mostly ignored it leaves one wondering why the TV is on in the first place! No one needs to be alone at home because the bar exists and it is open sometimes seven days a week from early morning till late at night.

A café, on the other hand is where you partake of a coffee and a pastry, or, when it's hot, a large ice cream. It is where you have a work break, read a newspaper, take shelter from the sun or rain, watch the world go by or even nip inside to use the toilet. In the city it is a haunt for all ages and sexes but in the country segregation takes place with the ladies visiting the café and the men the bar.

INTRODUCING WINE
Spaniards drink a lot. It is part of everyday life in which most people have a daily intake of alcohol. They may start the day having a coffee laced with brandy, take a bottle of red wine for lunch and sit in a bar all evening. But you only rarely see a drunken Spaniard. The prices of local wine sherries and brandies are very cheap and while whisky, gin or rum may be expensive in comparison, the measures are extremely generous.

The Spanish are casual in their attitude to wine. They do not take it seriously, drinking mostly young table wines. At the same price as a bottle of water, a carton of milk or a soft drink it is something that can be taken or left with a meal. In a restaurant, frequented by workmen having their lunch, half a bottle of unwanted red wine is frequently discarded. Wine is cheaper in Spain than in many other countries. A good quality Rioja only costs €3 and it has not increased greatly over the years.

Spain has a long history of wine production, with old stone wine presses still evident in the mountains. Storage in oak casks followed in the fifteenth century, but it was only in the 1960s that Miguel Torres established the first stainless steel wine-making equipment in his Catalán winery, giving precise control over the fermentation procedures. Most producers followed suit and now Barcelona is a world centre for the manufacture of wine-making equipment. This forward-looking attitude has given rise to a new approach to Spanish wine-making. After almost 2,500 years we can now enjoy the best of Spanish wines: nutty, dry and light, oaky reds with cinnamon depth, clean crisp whites, herby reds and new sparkling whites.

The extraordinary diversity of wines produced in Spain is not only due to the skill of the wine maker but to the country's different climatic and soil conditions. There are three main soil types: chalk, a bedrock called schist and clay. Chalk and schist provide water retention during the driest part of the year while clay is rich in trace elements such as iron.

There is a downside to Spanish wine. A lot of mediocre 'plonk' is still produced and it suffers from a poor international reputation. This has much to do with worldwide marketing skills as the quality of Spanish wine has improved enormously over the last few decades with the introduction of new grape varieties and more consistency in the processing. International varieties of grape are now grown such as Chardonnay, Cabernet Sauvignon, Merlot, Malbec, Pinot Noir and Riesling. They have joined the native varieties of Garnacha Tina, Graciano, Tempranillo, Albarino, Moscatel, Parallada, Pedro Ximenez, Verdejo and Xarel-lo.

CLASSIFYING WINE
The classification of wine is by law and label. It makes it easier for the customer to know what he is buying. There are three broad classifications covering Table Wine, Quality Wine and Ageing Wine. Table Wine is a European classification of basic quality of which there are four types.

◆ *Vino de Mesa* (VdM): a Table Wine blended from various regions. The label will state 'Vino de Mesa, Produce of Spain' and carry a brand name but no regional name and no date.

◆ '*Vino de Mesa...*': a Table Wine with the regional name inserted on the label, e.g. Vino de Mesa de Toledo.

◆ Vino Comarcal (VC or CV): a regional wine. There are 21 such classified areas. The label states 'Vino Comarcal...' followed by the regional name.

◆ *Vino de la Tierra* (VdIT): translated this is 'Wine of the Land', meaning country wine that is likely to apply for

Quality Wine status in the near future. The label will say 'Vino de la Tierra de...' followed by the district name.

Quality Wines meet European standards of quality control with each wine-producing zone made up of a council of growers, wine-makers, biochemists and government representatives. When a New Quality Wine is created by promotion from the VdIT standard a set of regulations is established, approved by the regional government, then Madrid and then finally in Brussels. There are two levels of classification.

- *Denominación de Origen* (DO). This is the main quality wine classification in Spain. There are 54 DO zones all tightly controlled. Regulations relating to a DO region include the type of grape that can be used, yield per hectare, minimum alcohol strength, permissible amount of natural sugar, the maturity process and period, bottling and labelling. The classification also has two labels. On the front is a label stating the name of the wine zone with the additional words '*Denominación de Origen*'. On a small back label is the official seal, a small map and the serial number of the bottle.

- *Denominación de Calificada* (DOCa). This is a higher quality of wine applicable from 1991 to the Rioja region. It guarantees wines that have performed to a high quality over a number of years through lower yields and grape selection. Labelling is the same as the DO category.

In addition to the classifications of brand name, producer's name, DO zone and the official seal Spain has its own system of classifying wines by age. What do they mean by age? Time in an oak barrel plus time in the bottle before being released for sale is the definition. There are five classifications:

- *Joven*: young wine – harvested one year and on sale the next – light and fruity.

- *Crianza*: six months (at least) in the cask and two years maturing.

- *Reserva*: three years maturing – with a minimum of one in oak and one in the bottle.

- *Gran Reserva*: from finest vintages – five years in the cellar of which two years are in the cask and three in the bottle.

- It should be noted that the time for age classification differs from red to white and rosé. White and *rosado* require six months in oak and can be released a year earlier than the red.

Spanish wine regions fall into four main areas: the north, where the best Spanish wines are produced, containing the regions of Galacia, Castile de León, Navarra, Aragon, Rioja, Catalonia and the Balearics; the central zone including La Mancha and Extremadura; Andalucia, the birthplace of Spanish wine, and the Canaries; and the coastal region of Valencia and Murcia, containing almost half of Spain's total vineyards. Spain has three climatic systems. Green Spain to the north, the climate of the

Meseta and the Mediterranean coast. The best vineyards, however, are situated in microclimates, on mixed soils, or on well-drained sheltered slopes.

To reiterate, the most famous Spanish red wine is Rioja, a strong wine with a distinctive oaky flavour gained from the time it spends maturing in an oak barrel. Few international wines can match Rioja, or its near neighbour Navarra, for price and quality. Pick up a wine list with offerings from all over the world and the name Rioja will appear.

The words Catalonia, Penedes region, microclimate, the Torres family, outstanding commercial success and good young wines at sensible prices say it all. Penedes is renowned for its white wines, although it also produces fine reds and much of Spain's premier sparkling wine.

Spanish sparkling wine is called *cava*. It is said that it is as good as French champagne but much cheaper. But more correctly it is a quality, young sparkling wine in its own right. Cava is identified by its sweetness or dryness and all *cava* wines come under the same DO irrespective of where they are produced.

SANGRIA, SHERRY, BRANDY AND OTHERS

Sangria is a summer drink. It is a fruit and wine punch diluted with lemonade. On occasions it may have the addition of some brandy to give it an extra kick. Care has to be exercised in buying sangria for it can be a place to 'lose' poor quality red wine. There is no way of knowing this but exercise care by always buying a branded product or purchasing at a reputable restaurant.

Sherries have always been popular. The English have dominated the sherry trade in Jerez de la Frontera in Andalucia where it's produced. Many of the brands are foreign, Harvey's and Sandeman to quote just two. Sherry is matured in oak barrels and produced from a variety of vintages by progressively blending young and old wines. There are various types of sherry to suit most tastes and occasions. Classic sherry is *fino* (dry) or *seco* (sweet). *Amontillado* is deeper in colour and taste and usually drank chilled as an aperitif. The very dry *manzanilla* is a fortified wine which has a slightly salty after taste, attributed to the salty soil of the area where it is produced.

Brandies make a perfect end to a meal. Some prefer *anis*, which is a Spanish aniseed drink rather like Pernod. But many more prefer the popular after dinner drink called *sol y sombre* (sun and shade), that is a combination of brandy and *anis*. It is not for the faint-hearted.

Beer is not generally what people think of when they think of Spain. They think of wine, sherry and sangria. Get ready for a shock. Spain's sales of beer surpassed sales of wine in the early 1990s. The most famous branded beer is San Miguel. It is quite strong (5.4%) and has a light, slightly sweet fruity taste to it. Cruzcampo is the closest you'll get to light beer without asking for it. It is a light and dry brew with a somewhat sour flavour.

Atlantic Spain grows a great quantity of apples that are fermented in chestnut barrels to produce cider, a tangy, light and mildly effervescent drink. Mass-produced it is available in dry and semi-dry varieties but natural cider, more like a 'home brew', is cloudier, fruitier and drank young.

VISITING THE *BODEGA*

Many people buy wine from the supermarket and hypermarket. The quality and range is good and, after all, there is always a 'special offer'. Supermarkets stock few imported wines. A *bodega*, which is a store selling only wine and drinks, usually has as large a selection as a supermarket. Look for a string of parked cars outside bodegas attached to a wine-producing unit. Large quantities of wine are sold straight from the barrel at ridiculously low prices.

SUMMARY

◆ The classic dishes of Spain are *gazpacho* soup, *paella*, *cocido* and sweet confectionery.

◆ Ham, dry cured for long periods, sausages, fresh fish, hard cheeses and fresh fruit and vegetables are in abundance.

◆ Regional food exists: fish and dairy products in the north, *crema Catalán* and *paella* in the east, barbecued meats in Andalucia, game and *cocido* in the centre of the country.

◆ Eating out is late, often very late.

◆ *Tapas* are unique to Spain.

◆ A bar is an environment to savour but not to linger in.

◆ The Spanish are casual in their attitude to wine. It is generally of good quality and cheap.

◆ Understand the classification of wine. It is worth the effort.

◆ Sherry and particularly brandy are other excellent Spanish drinks. *Sangria* is enjoyed by tourists.

◆ Surprisingly, beer sales are greater than those of wine.

(11)

Staying Young

ENJOYING A NEW LIFESTYLE

Moving to a new country calls for a change in outlook. It is a transition from one culture to another. For some it may be a shock. It is most important, however, to accept it as a different lifestyle. Adapt to it. Embrace the challenge and enjoy life.

About 12 million people whose native tongue is English will visit or reside in Spain in any year. The European Commission, in a survey, states that only 3% speak Spanish. A lack of command of a second language puts them at a severe disadvantage when communicating and integrating into the Spanish way of life.

The influx of foreign residents is not evenly spread throughout Spain. Some towns have developed as foreign enclaves. Denia, for example, has a high proportion of German residents. New urbanisations, when built, are marketed heavily in one country but not evenly across all countries giving rise to colonies of people who rarely understand the culture of Spain.

Of course there is sun worshipping and *cerveza* drinking but the novelty of that soon wears off since it can only lead to boredom or alcoholism, hopefully to be replaced with a more positive attitude to life, an attitude that says, 'Get out, learn about the country, develop new interests and meet new people.'

LEARNING ABOUT THE COUNTRY

The real way to learn about a country is to travel. There are other methods, such as reading books and tourist guides, which are colourful and informative. Watching travel films too has its place. But it is only by going to see a place that the true ambience can be experienced. Appendix 5 gives some suggestions of places to visit. It is by no means exhaustive. They are places where you can enjoy the sun, the sea and the mountains, places where you can benefit from the climate and keep in shape with your favourite all-year-round sport, where you can discover local history and monuments, travel down hidden byways and forest tracks, participate in local fiestas, meet local people . . . and much more.

Where else to go? Look no further than a good guidebook or the Spanish Tourist Information Offices.

ENJOYING SPORTING ACTIVITIES

The diverse geographical nature of Spain, with its mountains, woodlands, beaches and sea, provides a wonderful backdrop for sporting activities. Golf clubs, sports centres, bowling greens, gymnasiums, swimming pools, marinas and tennis clubs are all striving to make better use of our leisure time. The newcomer faces a bewildering choice of activities only handicapped by the ageing process, which probably rules out bullfighting, bungee jumping and hang-gliding. Football, rugby, running and hockey are now passive, spectator sports, as the battle with the waistline is probably lost. Similarly a short cycle ride to the supermarket seems to be more appropriate than dressing up each Sunday in matching bright lycra outfits, ripping calf muscles to shreds ascending narrow mountain roads astride the latest 21-gear machine.

No! It is time to put the more active stuff on the back burner. Slow down. Remember, this is Spain – where time is not important. Consider the less athletic pursuits where skill, knowledge and abilities can be honed to perfection with practice, practice and more practice. Golf and bowls perhaps. Tennis, or maybe hiking. Tone up at a gym. Take up fishing.

Golf
A hundred years ago, the screaming, jumping and beating of clubs on the ground was called witchcraft. Today it is called golf. Golf in Spain is booming, driven by tourism and the climate. The worldwide success of Ballesteros, Olazabal, Jimenez and Garcia has contributed to this success. Ballesteros is a star in Spain, an icon in Britain and if he had been Italian would by now have been painted on the ceiling of the Sistine Chapel.

The Costa del Sol is often referred to as Costa del Golf, such is the profusion of new courses. They are carved out of barren landscapes, pampered and watered to produce lush green fairways. Consequently golf is not cheap – €50 for a round is common. In Scotland, the home of golf, it is a game for the working man. In Spain it is a game for the tourist and the wealthy resident.

Plans are afoot to build 34 new golf courses on the Costa Blanca, which will bring supply and demand into balance. The water will come from the River Ebro in the north of the country under the National Hydrological Plan developed by the authorities to increase supplies for urban development, leisure activities and market gardening in the south-east of Spain.

The boom in Spain is in direct contrast to golf in the UK where they are feeling the pinch. Memberships are falling, joining fees are down by 42% and the number of rounds on municipal courses has fallen by 26%. Private clubs are rethinking their position and price (source – Golf Research).

Hiking

Walking or hiking clubs exist in all the main areas. For the adventuresome, the best places to go are the Picos de Europa in Northern Spain, the Pyrenees near the French border, the Costa Blanca inland from Benidorm and around the Sierra Nevada near Granada. Strangely, hiking is not too popular with Spaniards but is hugely popular with new foreign residents.

Many holiday companies offer Spanish walking tours. This has given rise to some excellent English-language publications describing good detailed routes with clear concise maps. The trails themselves are way marked, and the only hazards encountered are dogs and the unhygienic nature of some refuge huts. It is important not to underestimate some of these rugged trails with rapidly changing weather, snow on high ground and exposure on steep paths.

DID YOU KNOW?
All creatures great and small

Hikers should watch out for the Processionary Caterpillar Moth known in Spain as the *oruga*. The moths lay their eggs in white cotton wool like nests in pine trees easily visible from paths in the countryside. On hatching the caterpillars make their way to the ground in a nose-to-tail chain in search of the next place in their lifecycle. Don't touch them or poke at the nests or let animals near them. They cause a nasty rash and give off dust causing respiratory problems for adults. Children can become ill; cats and dogs have been known to die. The traditional natural antidote for the rash is vinegar, although olive oil and lemon juice are also recommended.

The only poisonous snakes found in Spain are vipers. They are very easy to recognise with a triangular head; they are a brown-yellow colour with a wavy black line down the spine and dots on the side. They measure 60 cm and avoid humans. Snakes are very active in warm weather, especially in the middle of the day and may be found basking on a rock. Be careful where you sit down. Do not move rocks and remember that snakes live in walls. The bite of a viper needs urgent medical attention.

Spain has a plentiful supply of honey. Indeed exclusive shops sell many varieties. In the country bees are best avoided. Small wooden hives, well signposted and located in sheltered warm places in the mountains are home to the honey-makers. Keep moving, leave the bees well alone.

Mosquitoes are annoying insects. A bite leaves painful, red, itchy blotches. Although in our latitudes any subsequent illness is moderated, the sting of the mosquito can cause problems for animals as well as humans. The females need to take blood to mature and begin laying in water 200 to 400 eggs. Therefore avoid abandoned containers, flooded gutters, puddles and water troughs that contain tepid water. On the other hand clean ponds with fish will eat the larva of the mosquito. Prevention is the main factor in controlling the population of mosquitoes. Eliminate stagnant water for it is indispensable to their reproduction.

Bowling

The capital cost to establish a bowling green is low. Demand is high. It is one of the few competitive sports for those of advancing years which combines well with social activities. Such is its popularity on the Costa Blanca that a winter league of nine clubs has a full page devoted to its activities in the local weekly paper.

Sailing

Adapting to the demands of a thriving tourist industry has led to the growth of pleasure craft harbours of which there are now hundreds stretched along the Mediterranean coastline. They range from small harbours that cater for a fishing fleet and dinghies to large, glitzy harbours such as Puerto Banus close to Marbella, which can cope with a thousand boats, many being no more than a display of wealth or floating gin palaces. It is hardly surprising that marinas are full to capacity but they do offer a full selection of services at a reasonable price. Customs authorities allow foreign registered boats to be used for six months of the year and to remain in the country for the rest of the year during which time the boat maybe used for habitation.

The development of marinas and new harbours has introduced spin-offs such as ships' chandlers shops, restaurants and bars and upmarket apartments. Yachting is for the rich with dinghy sailing for the rest of us. The Med can be choppy. Unfortunately there are not too many totally sheltered bays and regrettably even less supervised dinghy sailing clubs.

Fishing

So popular is fishing that the basic equipment is sold in supermarkets or newspaper shops. Sea fishing from the shore is still a sport for the youngster with only the smaller species being caught. River or lake fishing in Northern Spain is a far more serious matter altogether, with trout and salmon, pike and carp available. The local tourist office is the place to enquire about licences, season tickets and such like.

Tennis

Tennis is practised everywhere. It has been made popular by the many Spanish superstars. It is a low capital cost, highly popular activity. Every small town, hotel and club has its tennis courts utilised all year around. Many urbanisations, in addition to having a swimming pool, have a tennis court maintained through their community charge.

Running

It is not too hot to run! Spain, like all countries, has its runners and joggers. It has superstars too. It has often been host to international athletics meetings. Each town has its own sports ground complete with a running track. Marathons and half marathons are commonplace – but not in summer.

DID YOU KNOW
How to be a true Spaniard

He was lying face down, his head hanging off the bed, so when his eyes swam back into focus, jockeys, string vest and broken floor tiles were the first things he saw. In these waking moments he was unsure of where he was, a feeling of disorientation, what was happening? His mouth was full of dryness; a little man was banging hammers inside his head. He pulled on his running shorts, for a moment considered last night's vest, stepped into his still unclean Nikes, and ventured out into the bright sunlight, walking at first, then upping the pace to a very slow jog. Six miles later, having paused to urinate like a true Spaniard, he became a human being again, only being truly concerned about sleep starvation. Back home, standing in a pool of his former body weight, he removed his steaming trainers and damp shorts. Now he was a true Spaniard.

Gyms

Many privately run gymnasiums tend to be devoted to muscle building. But northern Europeans much prefer the weight reduction clubs of bright lycra, cardio-vascular training, running and cycling machines, saunas and steam baths. Modern gymnasiums exist, located in the many new building complexes.

Baring all on the beach

While France accepted nudism, it was not until the early 70s that topless sunbathing first appeared in Spain even although the patrolling Guardia Civil advised people to 'cover up'. Today it has changed with the practice common and nudism allowed in certain designated areas.

The first nudist resort appeared in 1979 near Estepona on the Costa del Sol but other beaches, about 60 in number officially designated with others that are not, are widely accepted as locations for naturism. There are four Naturist Associations.

Irrespective of what is worn, Spain now boasts the highest number of Blue Flag beaches and marinas in Europe. The Blue Flags are awarded where a high standard of water quality, environmental management, education, safety and the provision of services has been achieved.

Spain has 507 Blue Flags, France 339, Greece 377. The UK is in tenth spot with 128. Keep updated on www.blueflag.org.

Skiing

Ever heard of the Costa Blanca Ski Club? It sounds unreal. The Costa Blanca is sun, sea and sand! Literally hundreds of skiers travel from the Costa Blanca and all parts of Spain to the Sierra Nevada each year. It has several unique features as it is the most southernmost ski centre in mainland Europe and is also one of the highest giving a long season with good sunshine lasting until May. It is only 150 kilometres from the Costa del Sol and 400 kilometres from the Costa Blanca

Just outside Granada the resort is well developed with parking for thousands of cars and buses, 19 ski lifts capable of carrying 30,000 people per hour, 54 kilometres of marked slopes with 3.5 floodlit for night-time skiing at weekends and 17 hotels. Equipment hire and lessons present no problems – only doing it causes difficulties.

- The area is well named. – it is called *Solynieve* (sun and snow).
- Ski conditions telephone number 958249119.
- Road conditions telephone number 958282400.
- Accommodation telephone number 958249111.

Sports federations

There are many other sports available – squash, beach and water sports, horse riding, mountaineering, gliding, cycling and of course football, football and more football. Each sport has its own federation, which is always a good starting point for information.

INVOLVING YOURSELF IN SOCIAL ACTIVITIES

Social clubs are in abundance as ex-pats of similar nationality bond together around a common interest. In the *Costa Blanca News* there are hundreds of English speaking social clubs advertised weekly. You name it and it exists. Traditional clubs such as the Buffaloes, the Labour Club, the Conservative Club, the Bridge Club and the Solos Club are there. Many dancing clubs exist too such as line dancing, Scottish dancing, sequence dancing, Spanish dancing and Yellow Rock square dancing. Clubs such as the Computer Club, the Barber Shop Singers and the Gilbert and Sullivan Society compete for one's interest. For the physically active, there are walking and running clubs too. Pubs have quiz nights, restaurants theme nights.

Social clubs are a method of meeting people, of sharing a common interest, past or present. They are meeting places to deal with problems or to seek information. They are an aid to settling in a new country. Golf, hiking and bowls may be the top sports, but a meal, a drink or a visit to the club are the main social activities.

HOLIDAYING IN SPAIN

The traditional Spanish package holiday, still enjoyed by many, consists of sand, sea and sun. Holiday reps efficiently escort people from the airport to a three- or four-star hotel with half board accommodation, offer trips and sort out any problems. Going to amusement parks, having a good drink or cavorting with the opposite sex is everyone's idea of fun. This type of holiday will always be the core of Spain's tourist industry but it has now peaked. The boom in building new hotels has declined.

The Spanish holiday market is now segmented, firstly into different types of accommodation such as hotels, time-share and holiday homes, and secondly for special interest groups looking for a cultural, rural, walking or adventure holiday.

The new tourist concept is to develop Rural or Green Spain. It can be seen in national newspaper advertising and in promotional literature. The idea is to encourage tourists away from the Costas to rural areas without ruining the environment. There is much of interest in the country to commend it to the discriminating tourist. If successful it spreads revenue more equally across the country preventing the depopulation of rural areas.

Rural or green tourism goes hand in hand with rural

accommodation, developing local crafts, initiatives such as reopening disused railway lines and old stations, enhancing the facilities at the Nature Reserves and promoting the mountains for recreation. Yet another initiative lies in the development of spas. While there are over 300, many going back to Roman times, the majority have fallen into disuse.

Tourist information

Spanish tourist offices are excellent sources of information. They are well equipped with free publications and information. Offices exist in the city, town and airport or near a beauty spot. One very quick and effective method of obtaining information on accommodation, festivities and places of interest is simply to click on to each *comunidad*'s web page. Everything you could possibly want to know about a region is instantly available – in English, worldwide, before you even leave home.

Look at the following websites. These addresses use the name of the *comunidad*, the province or the town. There are many more. The letters .es are the Internet code for Spain. A good browser and the intelligent use of some key words will result in information from all parts of Spain suitable for a visitor or a new resident seeking to explore the country.

www.tourspain.es	the main Spanish tourist web site.
www.comunidad-valencian.com	a very good *comunidad* web site.

www.ayto-valencia.es 'ayto' is short for *ayunta-mienyo*, the town hall.

www.costablanca.org the Costa Blanca site.

www.xabia.org a popular town site

www.cullera-turismo.com a small site which even sends a CD-ROM.

SUMMARY

◆ The main sports for the ex-pat are golf, bowls and hiking. Most people do something.

◆ Social clubs are popular meeting places.

◆ The traditional Spanish holiday is changing. It is now Green Spain.

◆ Want some tourist information? Look at each *comunidad*'s web page.

Banking, Administration and Taxes

KNOWING BANKS AND CURRENCY

Walking down the *calle mejor* (high street) of any Spanish town you will notice the names of many banks are prominent. Caja Madrid, Caja Murcia, Banco de Santander and Banco Bilbao Vizcaya Argentaria (BBVA) are a few examples demonstrating the ability of each city to spawn its own bank. Incidentally the word *caja* means bank or till.

Banking in Spain is fragmented. There are about 150 different banks. They serve different markets and have different functions. Clearing banks, savings banks, lending banks, cooperative banks and some foreign banks of French, German or British parentage compete on an equal footing. These banks have many, many branches but caution is required, as naturally some of the smaller outlets do not offer a full range of services.

Make no mistake, while Spanish banking has some complicated procedures, it is reasonably efficient, usually staffed by friendly, hard-working, multilingual people capable of offering the customer some of the most up-to-date services including telephone, TV interactive and Internet banking.

Credit cards are issued for the purchase of consumer goods but sometimes only accepted with some other form of identification containing a photograph, such as a passport or ID card. The principal use of debit cards is to obtain cash, at a small charge, from an ATM (hole in the wall cash dispenser) of which there are many.

Opening a bank account is easy. The new chequebook has printed at the top the words *Cuenta en Euros de no Residente*. This indicates the Spanish banking system identifies separately residents from non-residents for tax purposes.

Anyone with a Spanish bank account will come across the practice of small, frequent statements. Monthly statements are not issued. After one or two transactions a statement is issued detailing when any standing order or direct debit occurred. A person with 12 normal transactions per month, including cash withdrawals, can expect four letters and probably 10 to 14 slips of paper. A special account, for, say a monthly mortgage payment can generate three slips transferring the money in and another three making the payment. The logic behind this is not clear. The banks think they are giving an excellent service. As with other things, one learns to adjust!

Strategic and offshore banking

The use of two accounts, one in the home country and one in Spain, should be enough for most needs. The transfer of money between the two is straightforward particularly if denominated in euros. For transfers between sterling and euros the use of an intermediate link, such as that provided by TAPS (the Bank of Scotland money transfer system) is cost effective.

Offshore banking has some advantages for investments and tax-free savings. The EU is trying to close such loopholes. Since Gibraltar is so close to the Costa del Sol it is still possible to bank 'offshore'. Many offshore current accounts offer cash or credit withdrawal worldwide. However a charge of 2.25% for exchanging pounds or dollars and 1.5% per withdrawal makes confidential offshore banking expensive.

The euro
Euro coins and notes have been circulating in EU member countries from January 2002. The much loved Peseta has now gone, held only in fond memories. At its launch the Euro instantly devalued but recently it has strengthened against Europe's other major currency, Sterling and equally against the mighty Dollar. Which currency is weak or strong is a matter of speculation.

Surprisingly the Eurocheque has also gone but euro travellers' cheques are available at any bank both inside and outside the euro monetary zone. European countries not participating in the euro tender are Denmark, Sweden and the UK. Of course Norway and Switzerland are not in the EU.

DEALING WITH RED TAPE
Spain has a reputation for red tape and bureaucracy which has its origins in duplicated decentralised government. At the local level, small 'stand-alone' administrative

offices deal with the everyday aspects of Spanish life. Little coordination takes place but one of the main focal points is the town hall (see Figure 11). The employment of a *gestor* will help deal with red tape and most people use his assistance until they become more familiar with administrative procedures.

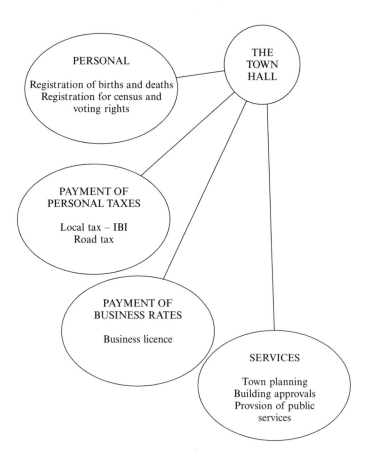

Figure 11. The town hall

Fiscal identification number

All residents or non-residents with financial dealings in Spain must have an identification number. This is called the *Número Identificación de Extranjero*. It is popularly called an NIE for short, the significant word *Extranjero* meaning foreigner. NIF, or *Número de Identificación Fiscal*, is the fiscal number which is the same as the NIE number. This serves as a fiscal identity and in the case of Spaniards, a passport number. It is easy to get an NIE, but long queues can be avoided by asking the *gestor* to complete this task.

- ◆ Visit the appropriate comisaria (police station).
- ◆ Take your passport with a copy, two photographs and complete the relevant form.

Signing on the *padrón* at the town hall

- ◆ Visit the town hall with your passport and the *copia simple* for the property.

- ◆ Complete some details. You are now on the census of inhabitants residing in the area administered by that particular *ayuntamiento*. (town hall)

- ◆ Persons registered will be allowed to stand and vote at elections.

- ◆ An *empadronamiento* certificate (census registration certificate) is issued.

Paying *impuesto de bienes inmuebles* (IBI) at the town hall

Popularly known as IBI this is a local tax levied on property value. It is effectively a local tax or rates payment. A receipt for the IBI payment will show the property's *catastral* reference number and the *valor catastral*, the assessed value of the property. It is necessary to visit the town hall to register the ownership of a property and to pay the IBI, for failure to do so results in a hefty surcharge.

The town hall is also the place to pay car tax (see Chapter 15).

Applying for *residencia*

If you intend to live permanently or to spend more than six months each year in Spain, then you must apply for a *residencia*. To do this visit the comisaria with the following documents:

- Copy of valid passport.

- NIE number.

- Three passport size colour photographs.

- The completed form.

Fingerprints are taken at the police station. In about six months a *residencia* card is issued. It is your new identity in Spain. It is renewable every five years. Your passport is only used for international travel. Revisit the bank to change your personal details and account numbers from non-resident to resident. Obtain a new driving licence (see Chapter 15). Most importantly it also means paying income tax to Spain and not from your home country (more details later in this chapter).

Entering the Spanish health system (INSALUD)

Temporary health cover administered through form E111 issued by European countries to cover illness on holiday or a short three-month visit is not an acceptable solution for Spain's new permanent residents. It is of course possible to take out medical insurance, which is the normal way of dealing with this issue. Emergencies, visits to the doctor and hospital are normally covered by this policy but medicines and dental treatment are not.

Disabled people and those over normal retiring age can gain access to the Spanish health system. They are entitled to the same medical treatment as back home. Visits to the doctor, prescriptions and hospital care are all free.

- Obtain form E121 from the Social Security office back home.

- Collate the *residencia* (or proof of application), the passport and a copy, and NIE.

- Go to the appropriate Social Security office to complete some paperwork.

- Go to the nominated administrative medical centre who will allocate a doctor.

DID YOU KNOW

The power of paper

Voting

Foreign nationals resident in Spain should not ignore the benefits incurred by signing on the *padrón* and thus gaining voting rights. It is now possible for foreigners to stand as councillors at local elections. In resort towns the number of foreigners now outweighs the number of Spanish. Germans, who have a talent for organisation, are keen to stand as councillors and they frequently do, ensuring that expenditure is properly targeted instead being spent in traditional ways such as improving the road to the *ermita*.

Keep all receipts

Always insist on a receipt, keep it and file it away. A complaint will not be entertained without a receipt. Keep records of taxes paid, bank statements, bills paid, guarantees and such like. They may never be required but in view of the Spanish love of paper, without documentary proof, there is little possibility of an issue being resolved. All payments to the town hall, all charges for motoring and all utility bill receipts should be kept. You never know when they will be required, but when they are it will invariably be to your benefit.

Customer service

All businesses in Spain are required by law to have a complaints book which must be produced on demand. This is a useful device if visiting a restaurant or a hotel as the owner does not wish to have entries in his book. In the event of a complaint about a product take the item and the receipt back to the supplier. It will be dealt with in the normal way. Failing that, complain to the *Oficina Municipal de Información al Consumidor* (OMIC) who have offices in liaison with the town hall. Large public service industries have appointed personnel to deal with complaints. Banks have an independent service with complaints being directed to *El Defensor de la Clientela*. Finally there is always the power of the *denuncia* (see Chapter 13).

MAKING A WILL

It is not absolutely necessary, but it is advisable, to have a Spanish will. A holiday homeowner or a foreigner, resident in Spain, is permitted to dispose of his Spanish assets according to the law of his home country under a valid will. The legal phraseology is that *he, or she is not domiciled in Spain.* Although Spanish inheritance rules differ from those of another country they are not normally applied, the law of the deceased's home country taking precedent. Spain's inheritance tax rules are, however, applied.

As it would take some time to administer a Spanish estate it is normally recommended that a Spanish will be written. The lack of a Spanish will prolongs probate on an English will. Legalising a will involves both the *abogado* and the *notario.*

LEARNING ABOUT TAXATION

Personal taxation is at the best of times complicated. In that context the Spanish taxman does not disappoint. As you would expect, the tax system is also ever changing. Most taxes in Spain are based on self-assessment where the individual is liable to report and calculate any tax due. Since we have difficulties doing this at the best of times the average new resident or non-resident, grappling with the language of the tax authorities, has little chance of getting this correct. Enter the *gestor* (see Chapter 7) who will not only perform these administrative tasks but may even suggest legitimate methods of tax avoidance.

Spain is not a tax haven. Its level of taxation is, however, generally low. The *Agencia Estatal de Administración Tributaria* collects government taxes but it is commonly called by its old name, *Hacienda*. The Spanish tax year is 1 January to 31 December. Tax returns must be presented between 1 May and the 20 June.

A non-resident spends less than six months per year in Spain. A Spanish resident is one who spends more than six months per year in the country, who has a *residencia* and has notified the tax authorities back home of their departure on form P85. This triggers entry into the Spanish tax system, which has a treaty with other European countries designed to ensure that income that has already been taxed in one country is not taxed again in another country. There is one important exception – a UK government pension is taxed in the UK, but not Spain.

To complete tax returns, some documentation is necessary.

- details of NIE number, address, age and marital status;

- proof of income;

- a year-end bank statement showing interest paid and average balance;

- a recent *Impuesto sobre Bienes Inmuebles* statement (IBI);

There are five main taxes administered by the *Hacienda* which the resident and non-resident will have to deal with. The rules differ from resident to non-resident:

- property taxes (*patrimonio* and *renta* tax);

- income tax (*impuesto sobre la renta de las personas físicas*);

- capital gains tax;

- wealth tax (*impuesto sobre el patrimonio*);

- inheritance tax (*impuesto sobre sucesiones y donaciones*).

Property taxes

A non-resident is liable for *patrimonio* and *renta* tax (wealth tax and unearned income tax). *Patrimonio* is calculated at 0.2% of either the property value as declared in the *escritura*, the rateable value or the market value, whichever is higher. *Renta* is nothing to do with renting out a property. It is a separate tax that is paid with the *patrimonio*, calculated at 25% of 1.1% of the rateable value of a property. It's a little bit complicated, but to give an approximation, allow half a per cent of the property value each year for both taxes.

A resident with only one property does not pay the *patrimonio* and *renta* tax but does so on second and subsequent properties.

Income tax – resident

Income tax is payable on both earned and unearned

worldwide income such as wages, pensions, property and investment income. A number of allowances and deductions can reduce the tax bill. These are mainly related to personal and general allowances which are related to age, dependants and disability, pension payments, mortgage repayments and charitable donations. Medical fees, medical insurance and school fees are not deductible.

Income tax – non-resident

Income tax for non-residents is simpler and more brutal. Income is taxed at a flat rate of 25% with no allowances.

Capital gains tax

Liability to capital gains applies to residents and non-residents. Capital gains are payable on the profit from the sale of assets in Spain such as property, stocks and shares, antiques, art and jewellery. Since most ex-pats will have arranged their investments free of tax, capital gains in practice should only apply to property. A capital gain is based on the difference between the purchase price and the selling price of the property, less the costs of buying and selling, and costs of improvement.

Residents

If the property has been owned for less than two years the gain is added to income and taxed accordingly. If the property has been owned for more than two years the gain is reduced by an inflation coefficient. Tax is payable at the individual's income tax rate with a fixed deduction before payment. For those over 65 years of age the gain is tax-free.

Non-residents

For non-residents the gain is taxed at a flat rate of 35%. The two-year ownership rule and inflation factor allowance still applies. Age exemption does not.

Wealth tax

Residents

Spanish residents are required to pay wealth tax on their worldwide assets less any liabilities. The assets are defined as property, vehicles, jewellery and investments and cash in hand at the bank. Liabilities include mortgages and other debts. The first €110,000 are free of tax (double that for a couple) and thereafter taxed on a sliding scale commencing at 0.2%.

Non-residents

Again harsher penalties accrue. They pay wealth tax at the same rate as residents on their Spanish assets but have no tax-free allowance.

Inheritance tax

Inheritance tax is certainly the most complicated of all taxes and needs specialised advice to legitmately reduce any liability upon death.

- ◆ Inheritance tax is payable if the recipient is a resident of Spain or the assets being passed on death are a property in Spain.

- ◆ Inheritance tax is paid by the beneficiaries and not by the deceased estate.

- Inheritance tax starts, on a sliding scale after a fixed allowance of €16,000 per recipient.

- The cornerstone of avoiding inheritance tax is to have a Spanish will for Spanish assets, good financial advice and the possible use of an inheritance trust.

There is no exemption between husband and wife for the joint ownership of a property. In many countries a property can be held in joint names. If one person dies the property passes automatically to the other person. This is not the case in Spain where each person holds an equal share, which upon the death of one person is subject to inheritance tax and succession law.

The value of a property can be reduced by 95% for the purposes of inheritance tax when the principal residence is bequeathed to a spouse, parent or child who has been living with the deceased two years prior to death and the inheritors own the property ten years from the date of death.

Yet another method of reducing inheritance tax is the peculiarly Spanish method of setting up a *usufructo* (a life interest). In this situation the ownership of the house is passed to the children leaving the life interest holders free to live in the property for the rest of their lifetime. Legitimate this may be, and easy to set up, but it is perhaps more suited to passing down the family home from generation to generation.

SUMMARY

- Spanish banks are modern and efficient but the frequency of statements can be irritating.

- Offshore banking is expensive.

- The first administrative step is to obtain an NIE.

- It is a requirement to sign on at the town hall for the national census, the main benefit being voting rights. The town hall is also the place for the payment of various taxes.

- Obtaining a *residencia* is a major change for a new resident to Spain. Your old identity is partly shrugged off. It has implications for income tax payments, changes to be made to bank accounts and the need to have a new driving licence.

- People who are disabled or over retiring age can enter the Spanish health system.

- Paper is power. Voting is democratic power. Threatening to fill in the complaint book is power.

- It is recommended that a Spanish will be made for Spanish assets.

- Everyone pays income tax. Capital gains, wealth tax and inheritance tax all have to be dealt with.

- One significant difference lies with the joint ownership of property. On the death of one person the share does not automatically pass tax-free to the other person.

Knowing the Institutions

UNDERSTANDING THE HEALTH SYSTEM

The Spanish are healthy people. A diet containing fish, fresh fruit and vegetables, olive oil instead of unsaturated fats and red wine contributes to this. The pace of life helps too. However, complaints associated with smoking-related ailments are high. Smoking is the leading cause of death among adults, with cheap cigarettes causing 55,163 deaths in the year 2001. Spain also has the second highest number of smokers in the EU.

For sufferers of rheumatism, arthritis and bronchitis, Spain's climate is therapeutic. The relaxed lifestyle has a positive effect on mental health since it is a well-known fact that people who live in sunnier climates are generally happier than those who live in cold, wet climates.

Spain has no special health risks apart from over-indulgence. The tap water is in the main drinkable, although during periods of shortage the quality may suffer and people revert to the bottled variety. Drink the red wine too, which is plentiful, cheap and beneficial to your health when consumed in moderation.

Doctors

The health care facilities are good. Medical staffs are highly trained and hospitals equipped with the latest technology. The public and private systems live happily together. The Red Cross also makes an important contribution. France and Germany lead the way in cost-effective health care but Spain, with the natural benefit of climate, spends less on health per head of population than its European partners.

Finding a doctor who speaks English can be a problem. In the public sector the doctors are Spanish and are unlikely to speak English. In the private sector, particularly in cities and resort areas, there are English-speaking German and Scandinavian doctors. Doctors advertise their services in the expatriate press.

With private health insurance you can choose a doctor from a list provided. Within the public sector the choice is more limited. Within the private sector specialists do not require patients to have a doctor's referral although this is necessary in the public sector.

Chemists

A chemist (*farmacia*) is recognised by the sign of a green-cross displayed outside the premises. The address of the nearest 24-hour pharmacy and a list of duty pharmacies is posted on a notice board and details are published in local newspapers. A pharmacist in Spain must own and run his own pharmacy. Pharmacy chains are illegal.

Private prescriptions cost 100% of the cost of the medicines. Prescriptions under the public health scheme cost 40% or nothing at all if for a pensioner or the handicapped. Prescription medicines are cheap but non-prescription drugs are expensive. General medication, such as aspirin or cough medicine, which can be purchased in supermarkets in some countries, can only be purchased in a pharmacy in Spain.

Chemists are highly trained and provide free medical advice for minor ailments. They are able to sell some remedies without recourse to a doctor. They can supply a wide range of medicines without a prescription.

Chemists only sell prescription drugs, non-prescription medicines, cosmetics, diet foods and toiletries. A *drogueria* sells non-medical items such as toiletries, cosmetics and household cleaning items. A *herboristeria* sells health foods, diet foods and herbal remedies.

Hospitals

Hospitales de la seguridad social (public hospitals) and *hospitales privados* (private hospitals) are the core of the health system together with establishments such as nursing homes, emergency clinics and analysis laboratories. Red Cross posts deal with minor accidents. Admittance or referral to a hospital or clinic for treatment is by a doctor or a specialist. Conversely it is possible to leave hospital at any time by signing a release form.

For private patients it is essential to provide evidence of health insurance or the ability to pay. If the private insurance company does not have an arrangement with the hospital to pay direct then the bill has to be paid by the individual and the cost reclaimed.

Spanish families are accustomed to looking after their relatives while in hospital and after they go home. Patients are still expected to convalesce at home, not in a hospital, and they are often discharged earlier than would be the case in many other countries.

Dentists

There are many good, private, English-speaking dentists. They are permitted to advertise their services and do so freely for it is a competitive business. Dentists expect to be paid after treatment is completed.

INSTITUTO NACIONAL DE LA SALUD

Public health benefits under the state health scheme called INSALUD (*Instituto Nacional de la Salud*), include general and specialist medical care, hospitalisation, laboratory services, medicines, maternity and some dental care. The emphasis is on cure rather than prevention.

Anyone who pays regular social security contributions is entitled, for themselves and family, to free medical treatment. The disabled, those on invalidity benefit and retired EU residents with a residence card who are in receipt of a state pension, also qualify. EU nationals of retirement age but not in receipt of a pension may be entitled to public health benefits.

Someone who has paid regular social security contributions in another EU country for two full years prior to coming to Spain is entitled to public health cover for a limited period. The home country administers this scheme.

If not entitled to public health benefits, private health insurance is necessary and proof must be presented when applying for a *residencia* card.

WHAT TO DO IN AN EMERGENCY

Emergency medical services in most EU countries, including Spain, are good. In a life-threatening emergency call for an ambulance and mention the nature of the emergency. The telephone numbers, which vary from province to province, are in the phone book, near the start, under the heading *Servicios de Urgencia*. Ambulances come under the umbrella of social security ambulances, Red Cross ambulances or 24-hour private medical centre ambulances. They are equipped with emergency equipment and staff are trained to provide first-aid. The ambulance service is usually free.

Taxis must, by law, transport medical emergencies to hospital when requested to do so. A private car can claim priority when transporting a medical emergency by switching on its hazard warning lights and waving a piece of white material from the window.

In an emergency, go to the hospital emergency or casualty department, or a 24-hour public health clinic. It may be important to check which local hospitals are equipped to deal with the situation. In an emergency a hospital must treat you, regardless of your ability to pay.

Visitors

EU residents visiting Spain can take advantage of health care agreements providing their home country has a reciprocal agreement with Spain. The UK does. EU residents should apply for a certificate of entitlement to treatment, known as form E111, from their local post office three weeks before planning to travel. The E111 is valid for three months only and must be validated by being stamped prior to departure. If the E111 is used for valid emergency or urgent medical treatment, present the form plus a photocopy to the medical practitioner or hospital that is providing the treatment. If payment is required obtain a receipt and apply for reimbursement back home.

DID YOU KNOW?
Emergency telephone numbers

Ambulance, Fire, Police	112
National Police	091
Telephone operator	1004

THE BEGINNING . . . AND THE END

Birth

Registration of a birth must be made within eight days at the local civil registry at the town hall or the hospital or clinic where the child was born. Registration applies to everyone irrespective of his or her nationality or residential status. There are two forms of birth certificate, a short certificate and a full certificate.

Unusually a birth certificate must state whether a child is legitimate or illegitimate (an illegitimate child is born less than 180 days after its parents' marriage or within 300 days of a divorce, annulment of a marriage or the death of the father).

Abortion is legal, tolerated in a liberal society and by the Catholic Church. It is currently available during the first 12 weeks of pregnancy in certain circumstances, e.g. when a pregnancy threatens the mother's life, the foetus is severely deformed or the pregnancy was the result of rape.

Marriage

To be married in a Roman Catholic Church in Spain at least one partner must be a Roman Catholic. A divorcee is not permitted to marry in a Spanish church if the previous marriage was solemnised in church.

In order for non-Catholic foreigners to marry one must have lived in Spain for at least two years. Marriages are held at Spanish civil register offices and are presided over by a judge, as church weddings for non-Catholics are not legally recognised.

Many British people find it easier to get married in Gibraltar, where the ceremony takes place in a register office in front of two witnesses. The colony has special regulations, which allow 'quickie marriages' by the Governor's Special Licence for non-residents. All you have to do is to prove you are not married to someone else, swear an affidavit at the register office, pay about €100 and collect the papers in two days.

Divorce

A couple must be married for one year before they can file

for separation and divorce by mutual consent. The separation must be legalised before a notary. After two years of legal separation the divorce is automatically granted.

The normal grounds for divorce are adultery, cruelty, desertion, mental disorders and alcohol or drug addiction. In these cases, where the separation is not by mutual consent, the period of legal separation is five years before a divorce is granted.

Foreigners who were married abroad can also be divorced in Spain if only one of the partners is resident.

Death

In the event of death, a certificate must be prepared and signed by the doctor who attended the death and legally certified by a judge. A death, like a birth, must be registered at the town hall of the district where it took place. If the deceased was a foreigner, the town hall will need a passport or *residencia* card. An international death certificate will then be issued. The death must also be notified to the deceased's local consulate or embassy in Spain. When a person dies several copies of the death certificate will be required for banks and the execution of the will.

A body can be buried or cremated or flown to another country for burial. A body cannot be interred sooner than 24 hours after death, but usually takes place within 48 hours, and if refrigeration is not available, within 72 hours. Although cemeteries in Spain are mostly Catholic, a person of any creed can be buried there. In most Spanish cemeteries, interment is above ground and bodies are placed in niches set into walls, which are rented for a number of years. After the rental period has expired, bodies are interred in a common burial ground within the consecrated cemetery grounds.

Many towns with a high proportion of retired foreign residents now have a crematorium. They operate in exactly the same way as those in the UK.

KEEPING WITHIN THE LAW

Spain has three main police forces, often with overlapping roles. They are the local municipal police, the national police and the Civil Guard. Some regions, including the Basque area and Catalonia, have their own police forces. An elite Special Operations group is responsible for combating terrorism and guarding Spanish ambassadors and embassies abroad. Other forces include the port police and armed guards employed by banks and security companies.

Municipal police

The municipal police are attached to local town halls in small towns. They wear blue uniforms with white chequered bands on their hats and sleeves and patrol in white or blue cars. Municipal police deal with minor crime such as traffic control, protection of property, civil disturbances and the enforcement of local laws.

National police

Stationed in large towns they deal with serious crime such as robbery, murder and muggings. Other duties include guarding embassies, railway stations, post offices and army barracks and controlling demonstrations. They are housed in conventional police stations some of which have an *extranjeros* (foreigners) department dealing with *residencia* cards and other matters relating to foreigners.

Civil guard

The *Guardia Civil* patrol Spain's highways often in pairs on motorcycles. They mainly deal with traffic offences and road accidents, but also act as immigration officers and frontier guards. In villages too small for the national police, the *Guardia Civil* stand in for all duties.

The *denuncia*

If you have a complaint against someone, usually a neighbour encroaching on your land (probably German), making too much noise (probably Spanish) or creating smells (probably French), you can make an official complaint. It is called a *denuncia* and is made to the *Guardia Civil*. The form, called the *Certificado de Denuncia* is completed with an official stamp. It may take time, but the complaint will be investigated. The *denuncia* is a good Spanish custom.

In the event of theft or loss of property a police report is required within 24 hours in order to reclaim this loss from an insurance company. The report is again the *denuncia*. In large cities and tourist areas where theft is common or pickpockets operate, it seems to be the policy to have a translator on hand at police stations to offer help.

Driving offences

The Spanish police are generally tolerant and extremely helpful. If you need the police, ambulance or fire brigade, try to engage the help of a nearby Spaniard since the person answering the phone is unlikely to speak English.

Of course it is to be hoped that no such problems will arise and the worst encounter might be a fine for a traffic offence. If this happens the police will fill in a short report and fine you on the spot. Drivers must have personal identification, driving licence and all car documents to hand (or copies). Some people resent carrying such valuable documents in a car and you may well be excused for not carrying them. But it is illegal to be without them and it can be a real nuisance if the police insist on seeing them.

Remember it is illegal for anyone to be without some form of personal identification and a *residencia* card or passport should be carried at all times.

SUMMARY

- The Spanish are a healthy people. Spain is a healthy country to live in.

- The medical facilities are good and the medical staff well trained. The public and private systems exist happily together.

- Chemists are highly trained and provide free medical advice for minor ailments.

◆ Hospitals tend to discharge patients early for home convalescing.

◆ Pensioners from the EU can enter the state medical system called INSALUD.

◆ In an emergency... just go to the hospital. They will treat you free of charge.

◆ Visitors should obtain reciprocal treatment by using form E111.

◆ There are three, usually tolerant, often overlapping police forces.

◆ Do not forget the *denuncia*, a helpful aid for sorting out neighbours and a must for reporting theft.

The Shopping Experience

FORGET MARKS & SPARKS

Spain does not have the equivalent of a Boots, Marks & Spencer, Dixons, W.H. Smith or J.J.B. Sports. The Spanish shopping experience is absolutely different with specialist small family-run outlets forming the bulk of sales activity.

Why is there a difference between Spain and the multiple retail outlets of Northern Europe? Well, remember it is a large country with a low population density, which in turn gives rise to high distribution costs. The nature of retailing has as a consequence many small outlets, with high price points and little discounting. Having said that, in the city things are changing to a more European approach with numerous out of town shopping centres being built to retail sporting goods, domestic goods, electronics, computers and clothing.

Tiendas

The smaller *tiendas* (shops) are cheerful, friendly, helpful places with the owners and assistants anxious to please. It is also where the annoying Spanish characteristic of 'not forming queues' is seen at its worst. People push and shove to the front to be served. This is best dealt with by patience as the perpetrators of this behaviour are often elderly who seem to think that their advanced years entitle them to non-queuing privileges. Alternatively say *perdone* and address the sales assistant who usually knows what is happening.

Opening hours for *tiendas* vary between summer and winter, but normally are 9.30 am to 1.30 pm and 4.30 pm to 7.30 pm Monday to Friday, plus a Saturday morning. The afternoon *siesta* seems inappropriate in winter but essential in summer when the shops open later, as no one wishes to go shopping during the intense heat.

Bread shop	–	*la panadería*
Butchers	–	*la carnicería*
Cake shop	–	*la pastelería*
Chemist	–	*la farmacia*
Clothes shop	–	*la tienda de ropa*
Delicatessen	–	*la charcuteria*
Fruit shop	–	*la frúteria*
Fishmonger	–	*la pescaderia*
Grocer	–	*la tienda de comestibles*
Hairdresser	–	*la peluqueria*
Ironmonger	–	*la ferreteria*
Laundrette	–	*lavandería*
Newspaper stand	–	*el quiosco*
Shoe shop	–	*la zapatería*
Travel agent	–	*agencia de viajes*
Tobacconist	–	*el tabac*

Hypermarkets
French-owned hypermarkets such as Carrefour and Intermarché dominate food retailing. Smaller German

supermarkets such as Lidl and Aldi compete on price but not on product range. Spanish companies, such as Mercadona and Masymas, are now gaining a solid foothold. Hypermarket shopping is an experience not to be missed, with everything possible to buy being sold beneath one roof. Clothes, footwear, garden plants and equipment, sports goods, bicycles, electrical goods, hi-fi, furniture, DIY, motoring accessories, kitchenware, toys and books are all sold. The food hall has a massive product range. The fruit and vegetables are highly colourful. The delicatessen counter is staggering in its variety of sausages and cheese, and the fish counter is laden down with salmon, trout, mussels, skate, mackerel and a whole range of unrecognisable species. The wine, spirits, soft drinks and bottled water section stretches for miles. These hypermarkets have forty to sixty checkouts. Key staff are even equipped with roller skates to get from point to point. Franchised within the same building are restaurants, banks, jewellers, newsagents and the National Lottery.

Clothing

Regrettably there is only one major, but famous, clothing chain store in Spain – El Corte Inglés. It has a similar marketing style to other European retailers selling male and female clothing together with books, CDs, electrical goods, computers, kitchenware and sports equipment. Price points are similar to or higher than the rest of Europe with only occasional sales (*rebajas*). With the exception of a large number of international sports brands, Spanish clothing is not fashionable. In fact it is conservative, with citizens sticking to fairly traditional styles.

European chain stores, like European banks, have only a few outlets in major cities. The marketplace may be penetrated by individual foreign brands but not by foreign retailers. Where they do exist they tend to be a poor relation of their national parents. But things are changing. Small fashionable chains are opening – Springfield for men's clothing, Corefield for women's fashion, Sprinter for active sporting goods. The *tiendas* and El Corte Inglés are at last having some competition.

Open air markets

There is a profusion of mobile open-air markets often stopping normal activity in a town for one day of each week. People flock from kilometres around to buy hams, fresh fruit and vegetables but not fresh fish. Clothing too is sold together with some ceramics and leather goods. Beware of purchasing designer items, watches and jewellery as they may be fakes.

Bargaining can take place, but it is an unnatural custom for Northern Europeans. Want to bargain? Express an interest in an item. Haggle on price. Say 'no' and walk away. The stall owner comes after you. That's when you get the low price, not before.

The hustle and bustle can be of some interest, but be cautious. Pickpockets, operating in gangs of two or three, are often present at open-air markets.

Mercado central

The local council runs the indoor central market. Most towns have one. They are efficient, clean, hygienic purveyors of fish, meat, pastries, fruit and vegetables, a traditional alternative to supermarket shopping. Little English is spoken. Most of the goods on display are home grown and throughout the year there is a wonderful selection. The market has to be first choice for freshness.

Shopping in Spain, with its markets in most towns and villages, is a happy, friendly experience. The choice and quality is high, it is colourful and healthy. For the shopper the exercise of buying is a real pleasure. Usually a stall is playing some music creating an atmosphere of 'fun time' in a festive and very Spanish way.

Food from home?

Bread can come in all its various guises. A fresh Spanish 'barra.' A French baguette. Bread from the UK, Germany and Holland is also available. The traditional English loaf is made under licence in Spanish bakeries.

Spanish cheese is good and supplemented by popular cheeses from the rest of Europe. Lovers of cheese soon branch out and try different Spanish cheeses. They find they can survive without Cheddar though this is readily available.

Any large conurbation of Northern Europeans will invariably have supermarkets meeting their demand for well-known food products that apparently they cannot live without. Freezers contain gammon steaks, bacon, English sausages, steak and kidney pies and so on... and German products too.

Imported, long-life, tinned or dry products are freely available... soups, pastas and such like. They come in a branded wrap, such as Baxter's, John West or even from Tesco or Waitrose. We are grateful.

The soft drinks market is truly international. Spanish milk is mainly long-life in a bewildering range. Fresh milk is available. So too is fresh coffee at a reasonable price, though English tea is expensive.

SHOPPING ABROAD

If you live in Spain, why not shop in Andorra, France, Portugal, Morocco or Gibraltar? Disadvantages may be these countries are some distance away and if the goods are faulty they may have to be returned to the place of purchase. Advantages are the euro and the credit card, which have assisted cross-border spending.

The tax-free shopping havens are Gibraltar and Andorra. Andorra is close to France attracting visitors of many nationalities. Electrical items are the most popular but do not expect the sales assistant to explain the product, just to take the money. Cheese and other foodstuffs are good buys. It can be a long way to go for a bargain but not so onerous if combined with a skiing trip. Gibraltar too is the home of tax-free electrical and liquor stores.

BEST BUYS

Wine

The best buy in Spain is undoubtedly wine from a tightly regulated industry. It is cheap and the quality good.

As we have seen in Chapter 10 Spain produces excellent wines but their product marketing has been poor leaving France holding the premium market and Spain operating at the bottom end. Tighter government regulations have seen a continuous rise in wine quality but not in their marketing strategy.

At an identical cost to a soft drink or a bottle of water, it is a natural accompaniment to a meal. Branded wine, with an individual number on the back of the bottle, blended house wines, *vino de mesa* (table wines), young wines or supermarket brands at up to €3 per bottle are all exceptional value for money.

Olive oil
There are 400 million olive trees in Spain with 80% grown in Andalucia. Driving around Córdoba and Granada it is possible to see fields and fields, acres and acres of olive trees but the experts in Brussels say there are too many – olive oil production is too high. *Aceite de oliva* (olive oil) is used in cooking, as a salad dressing and as a substitute for butter and margarine.

It is a sad fact that olive oil consumption in Spain has dropped in recent years. Compared to other forms of oil such as corn and sunflower it is expensive to produce as it is labour intensive. Picking olives by hand compares unfavourably with mechanised farming methods employed elsewhere. It has been said that olive oil contributes to a good complexion, efficient digestion and strong hearts. It is probably true, as olive oil contains little cholesterol.

The Romans first introduced olive trees to Spain and the best olive oil is still sent back to Italy and then re-exported. However, the 1,000-year-old drought and fire resistant trees remain. So too do the harvesting methods which consist of shaking the tree and picking up the olives from a net on the ground. Green olives are harvested in September and black ones in December.

Most of the olives picked are pressed for oil. The label on the bottle should be examined for the acidity and the number of pressings. Virgin extra is from olives picked ripe and pressed immediately and contains a maximum of 1% acidity. Virgin *fino* is up to 1.5% acidity. Virgin *corriente* is up to 3.3%. Virgin *lampante* is strong oil with little taste and an acidity level above 3.3%. The higher the acidity, the stronger the flavour and the lower the price. *Aceite de oliva refinado* is virgin oil whose taste or acidity makes it unsatisfactory but once refined it is still a healthy usable product. *Aceite de oliva* is a blend of both refined and virgin oils, this being the overall market standard.

It is a tightly regulated industry giving a consistent quality product and follows practices similar to the wine industry by issuing *denominación de origen* labels.

Saffron

Saffron is one of the best buys in Spain. Look to see that all the threads are of uniform length, are a deep burnt orange colour and the aroma is of the genuine article. Because of its extremely high market value saffron has always tempted fraud. Ground saffron is easy to replicate with turmeric or saffron simulators.

Ceramics

A *regalo* is a gift or a present. They are sold in tourist souvenir shops of the same name and in household furnishing shops. Spanish *regalos* are ornate rather than simple, decorative rather than functional, the ceramics, lighting and ornaments often being used to decorate a traditional home. Ceramics in particular are decorative, bright and colourful.

Leather goods

They may be made in Mallorca or mainland Spain or imported from Morocco. Each point of origin results in quality leather goods. Handbags, travel cases, belts or clothing all represent good value for money.

Tobacco

If wine and olive oil are good for you then cigarettes are certainly not They are purchased at yet another national institution – the *tabac*, the state-owned tobacco shop which sells all brands of cigarettes, cigars and tobacco at low prices – €20 for 200 cigarettes is quite normal. It is fairly obvious from these prices many people still smoke.

Have you ever been stopped by someone offering to sell you a carton of cigarettes at a ridiculously low price? Wondered about it? They are cigarettes made in the USA, imported into Gibraltar and then smuggled illegally into Europe through Spain. It is no secret. The imported price is about €10 for a carton of 200 cigarettes compared to double that price in Spain and a fraction of the price in Northern Europe.

DID YOU KNOW?
Wasted water

Crop irrigation takes place through a complex system of stone or concrete channels to gravity feed water from tanks to cultivated fields. A series of doors, open or closed within the channels, diverts water to various locations. The system has remained unchanged for centuries. Orange and lemon trees are watered once or twice per week by flooding the groves. It is a very inefficient system. The hot sun immediately evaporates the water. It takes millions of litres of water to supply a field for one year.

On the plains of La Mancha things do get slightly better. Massive sprays water the long rolling wheat fields. But evaporation there too is a problem.

What does this all mean?

There is more water consumed per head of population in Spain than in any other European country. This is a remarkable statistic. However most of this commodity is used in agriculture leaving drinking water in some coastal areas both scarce and impure. Desalination plants are constantly being built. City mayors fight for supplies as irritated voters register their displeasure at having to buy bottles of *agua* because tap supplies are undrinkable.

The farmers in Arizona do it better. They have pipes located about 20 cms under the surface of the soil drip feeding water to the roots of plants for a few minutes per day. Water is conserved. It does not evaporate.

Spain has a long way to go in conserving water. However the oranges and lemons are very juicy.

PURCHASING UTILITY SUPPLIES

Teléfonica, the Spanish telephone company, is a major communication organisation within Europe. It has a good reputation for service and efficiency with consumer prices similar to other European countries. Greater competition exists within the mobile phone market.

Iberdrola, the Spanish electricity supply company, is not quite so reliable. It is not unusual to have disruptions to supply and the service can be slow. The high unit prices are decreasing.

Gas supply is by bottles, or on large urbanisations from a central supply point. The service is good but, due to the door-to-door distribution system, very labour-intensive and erratic.

In practice there is little choice with land-line phones or electricity, gas and water supplies. You have to buy what is available and that is usually from only one supplier. However, EU governments are seeking to open competition in this area.

SUMMARY

♦ The backbone of the shopping experience is small family-owned shops called *tiendas*.

♦ Hypermarket shopping is available with these outlets stocking everything it is possible to buy under one roof.

♦ Fashion and clothing outlets are slowly facing more competition from newer small chain stores.

♦ Open-air markets, the central market and the *tabac* are other traditional outlets.

- ◆ It is possible to buy foods from home... and from Germany too.

- ◆ Try the tax-free havens of Andorra and Gibraltar for an unusual shopping experience.

- ◆ Wine, olive oil, ceramics, saffron, tobacco and leather goods are best buys in Spain.

- ◆ Water is wasted.

- ◆ There is little choice when purchasing utility supplies.

(15)

Travel and Communications

TRAVELLING BY ROAD

Roads

Spain's motorways are known as *autopistas* or *autovias*, both characterised by blue signposting and built to a high standard. *Autopistas* are toll roads. Other roads in Spain are identified by the sign *Red de Carreteras del Estado* (the red roads of the country), the *Carreteras Nacionales* (letter N on maps), and the narrower *Carreteras Comarcales* (letter C) often taking traffic more suited to the expensive *autopistas*.

On major roads each kilometre is marked with a number indicating the kilometres radiating from Madrid. In the provinces it is the distance from the provincial capital. These kilometre markers are often used as convenient meeting points or used to establish the location of a building.

On-the-spot fines are handed out for breaking speed limits, which are:

Autopistas	120 km/h
Autovias	120 km/h
Carreteras Nacionale	90 km/h
Carreteras Comarcales	60 km/h

Gasolina (petrol), *gasoleo* (diesel), and *gasolina sin plomo* (unleaded petrol) is available everywhere at prices well below average for other European countries. Indeed diesel is only about 60% of the most expensive European price.

The numbers of filling stations are increasing at about 4% per year. They additionally sell newspapers, food and snacks. Motorway services are poor and infrequent and generally recognised as the worst in Europe.

Driving on the right side of the road

The most obvious motoring difference is of course left-hand drive cars and driving on the right-hand side of the road. There are other important differences.

- When going around roundabouts in an anti-clockwise direction in some situations the occupant of the roundabout does not have the right of way.

- On a major road it is possible to change direction when the sign *Cambio de sentido* appears.

- When turning left at a busy junction, it may be necessary to turn right first and then cross the carriageway.

- Two flashing amber lights means, 'slow down, danger ahead'.

- Respect the narrow inside lane – it is for scooters.

- Seat belts are compulsory.

- All vehicle documents, such as insurance details, car registration and technical ITV (the equivalent of UK

MOT) sheets, should be kept in the car for inspection by the police if necessary.

Accidents

Spain is a big country. Driving on the wide-open motorways is a pleasure. Unfortunately Spain has one of the highest accident rates in Europe. A high incidence of foreign drivers is one significant reason. Poor roads and alcohol are other major reasons. One further characteristic stands out – speed. Spanish drivers are similar to the Italians and drivers on the Paris ring road – they all drive in a fast, aggressive manner. At slip roads, where they join major roads, no quarter is given or asked by the incoming drivers. Slipping into a small gap between traffic moving at high speed can be quite frightening.

In rural areas, holiday locations and areas with tolerant policing, bad driving and dangerous parking occur. Drivers stop their cars to talk to a passerby. Parking restrictions are ignored. This attitude is best summarised as below:

In Madrid, traffic lights are instructions.
In Alicante, traffic lights are suggestions.
In Pedreguer, they are Christmas decorations.

Dangerous roads

The N340 is a four-lane highway with no central reservation and runs the full length of the Costa del Sol from Málaga to Estapona. It was dubbed the most dangerous road in Europe. Hundreds of lives were lost each year as pedestrians tried to run across four lanes of traffic because there were no footbridges.

Things have improved. A new *autopista* has been built. It has flyovers, pedestrian bridges, tunnels and very steep gradients along its spectacular route. It is still, however, a dangerous road around Málaga and Marbella where the volume of traffic, excessive speed and short slip roads cause hazards.

A few kilometres north of Alicante on the A7 *autopista* is the San Juan tunnel, one of the five most dangerous in Europe. An EU investigation found that the 1,840 metre tunnel, built in 1990 and used by 50,000 vehicles per day, poses a serious threat to user safety because it lacks many basic safety features such as closed circuit television, fire detection systems, automatic alarms, emergency lighting, illuminated escape routes, congestion detectors and fire hydrants. Tunnel safety is classified as 'very poor'.

Imported cars

Driving a foreign registered car temporarily in Spain requires a green card, a bail bond, a national identity sticker on the back of the car, two red triangles, spare bulbs and a first aid kit. The headlights may need to be adjusted.

Purchasing a car (*el coche*)

The marketplace for the purchase of new cars is similar across Europe. Large dealers sell new and some second-hand cars at very competitive list prices with a good after-sales service. Since dealerships are monitored by the car manufacturers the service is efficient, well organised and, above all, reputable.

Product pricing is affected by discounting or special offers directly from the manufacturer. Look for new car discounts of 10% to 20% from the pre tax list price. Dealers quote one price for a new car inclusive of all taxes and on the road costs. It normally includes metallic paint and air conditioning as standard.

Given Spain's geographical location and the ownership of car manufacturing plants in Valencia, the popular brands are Seat and Ford. French products come next. Quality German cars are popular. The market penetration of small Far Eastern cars is high.

Regrettably the second-hand car market does not enjoy a good reputation with the usual unsavoury dealers in evidence, some of whom are British. Fortunately the quality of a modern second-hand car is high. It is price, poor administration, a lack of customer service and dishonesty which gives this market its poor reputation. The market for second-hand cars is unusual. A large number of one-year-old rental cars with relatively low mileages are sold through the second-hand market each year. Trade-ins from new dealership purchases are also sold through second-hand outlets. Cars are also offered for sale through the small ads in weekly newspapers. For a first-time buyer in Spain the advice is to tread carefully. The risk of a poor product or incorrect paperwork is great.

Insurance

Insurance companies offer the usual cover with options such as voluntary excess, no claims bonus and passenger insurance. One good additional extra is breakdown insurance, which provides for transportation of the car and occupants in the event of breakdown or illness.

MEETING MOTORING REGULATIONS

The Spanish traffic department is known as *Tráfico*. It has a reputation for having difficult and complex procedures. It is the worst example of Spanish bureaucracy. Most people use a *gestor* to deal with motoring regulations.

Driving licence

After obtaining a *residencia* there is a requirement to change your old licence for a new Spanish one. A recent EU regulation does not make this obligatory, and you may wish to continue to use your foreign driving licence registered and over-stamped in Spain. But it has an old address and if you are a new resident of Spain it is better to have a Spanish driving licence. If anything goes wrong it makes life just that little bit easier.

- Go to the information counter at the local provincial traffic department (*Jefatura Provincial de Tráfico*).

- Complete an appropriate form (*Solicitud de carnet del permiso de conducir*) and present the residency card and a photocopy, the old driving licence and three passport style photographs.

- The licence is not for life. It is renewable every few years according to age. A medical examination may be necessary, carried out at an approved centre.

Road tax

All Spanish registered vehicles must pay road tax (*impuesto municipal sobre vehículos de tracción mecánica*). The tax is based on the horsepower of the car. The tax levels are set by individual municipalities and can vary from town to town.

Payment is to the local town hall during a published time window after which a surcharge is applied. Unlike many other countries a tax disk is not placed inside the windscreen. Some people have avoided paying this tax for years but it catches up with them when a copy of the last receipt is required upon selling or scrapping the car.

Buying and selling

In order to buy a car in Spain it is necessary to have an NIE, a *copia simple* for your house, a property rental agreement or a *residencia*. When buying a new car a registration tax of 7% to 16% is levied. When buying a second-hand car a transfer tax, which reduces annually, is levied according to the age and engine size of the vehicle.

A simple agreement should be drawn up to sell a car. It should contain factual details of the buyer, the seller, details of the car, price and form of payment, the date and the appropriate signatures. It is stamped at *Tráfico* to exempt the seller from future fines, accidents or taxes.

There is a two-part vehicle registration, one for the details of the car and one for details of the owner. The details of the car do not alter but the part giving details of the owner alters each time there is a change. This document is called the *Permiso de circulación*.

It is customary when buying or selling a car to leave the administration to a garage or a *gestor*. The registration documents have to be altered, taxes paid, the town hall notified and *Tráfico* informed.

ITV (Technical Inspection of Vehicles)
After three years a bi-annual vehicle inspection, known as an ITV, is necessary. When the car is passed a sticker is placed inside the windscreen. After ten years it is an annual inspection.

TRAVELLING BY TRAIN
The state-owned company *Red Nacional de los Ferrocarriles Españoles* (RENFE) operates the Spanish rail network consisting of 15,000 km of track and 2,500 stations. The network covers all major cities and is supplemented by a few suburban networks and private narrow-gauge railways. Compared with the volume of goods shipped by road, little freight is transported by train. Like the UK, the railway system is underfunded.

RENFE operates a service that is continually improving. The fastest services are called the AVE and the TALGO, their names being acronyms for the high-speed trains that run along these routes. *Grandes Lineas* (long distance), *regionales* (regional) and *cercanias* (local) are other, self-explanatory, marketing names.

Madrid and Barcelona stations
The Spanish railway system is centred on Madrid, from where three main lines radiate out to other parts of the country. Consequently there are good links between Madrid and other cities. It is, however, difficult to get

from one regional capital to another without going through Madrid.

Madrid has three main stations.

♦ Chamartin serves Albacete, Alicante, Barcelona, Bilbao, Cádiz, Cartagena, Córdoba, Málaga, Santander, Seville, Zaragossa and France.

♦ Atocha serves Castilla-La Mancha, Almeria, Andalucia and Extremadura, including, Cádiz, Ciudad Real, Córdoba, Cuenca, Granada, Salamanca, Toledo, Valencia and Portugal.

♦ Principe Plo serves Coruña, León, Lugo, Ovense, Oviedo, Salamanca and Valladolid.

The main stations in Barcelona are Franca and Sants. Trains to all major Spanish cities and to France leave from Sants, while Franca has daily international trains, called the TEE (Trans European Express) to Geneva, Milan, Paris and Zurich. At border stops it may be necessary to change trains due to Spain's wider gauge of 1.676 m compared to 1.435 m for the rest of Europe

The AVE and Talgo network

The introduction of the AVE (*Tren de Alto Velocidad Española*), which also means 'big bird' in Spanish, utilises French and German technology by running on special lines and traveling at speeds of up to 250 kph. It has improved rail travel in Spain. Using the same gauge as the rest of Europe, the routes to Seville, Huelva, Cádiz, Málaga and Algecerias from Madrid are now operational.

Routes to Portugal, France, Barcelona, Valladolid, Bilbabo and Valencia are planned. The AVE and the slightly slower TALGO system will eventually comprise part of a European, high-speed rail network.

Other services

Grandes Lineas are air-conditioned intercity trains of a high standard operating between major cities with services including waiters with trays of airline style meals. *Regionales* are again modern trains. There are suburban services to all large cities. *Interurbano* is the Spanish equivalent of the suburban line. A metro system operates in Madrid. Business people still rarely commute to work by train; the car is still the preferred means of city transport, which helps to explain city traffic jams.

There are also a variety of slow, local and short-distance trains. The *exprés* is a slow night train, usually with sleeping cars, and the *rapido* is a daytime version of the same. Despite the names, the *exprés* and *rapido* are not particularly fast. Night trains (*estrellas*) are slow trains with a choice of *literas* (compartment with six bunk beds, or a *cochecama* (compartment with two beds).

Special trains

The Costa Blanca Express runs frequently from Denia to Alicante (two hours for 93 km). The Lemon Express runs between Benidorm and Gata de Gorgos on the same track. Gata is visited for its famous guitar factory and its wicker basket shops.

In Majorca it is still possible to enjoy a trip on a vintage train running from Palma to Soller. It travels through tunnels and mountains and provides some of the best views on the island. From Soller an equally ancient tramcar runs through orange and lemon groves to Puerto de Soller.

The *Al Andalus Express* is a unique travel experience on a luxuriously converted 1920s train with the six day round trip commencing in Seville and taking in Córdoba, Granada, Málaga, Ronda and Jerez. The sleeping cars and suites were built in France in 1929 for the King of England.

El Transcantabrico is another 1920s train operating between Santiago de Compostela and San Sebastian in northern Spain along a long stretch of narrow-gauge railway. It takes in stunning mountain scenery and offers excursions to a number of villages and towns during its week-long journey.

Tickets and fares

AVE, TALGO and Grandes Lineas tickets can be booked at the station ticket office or by travel agents. Local and regional tickets are available from the station booking office and ticket machines. RENFE operate a variety of trains, all with a different speed, service, classification and fare structure. Train travel may be fast or slow, the service good or leaving much to be desired, but Spanish fares are low by European standards. An example of a Spanish timetable is shown in Figure 12.

Origen: VALENCIA					Destino: OLIVA	
H. Salida	**H. Llegada**	**Desde**	**Hasta**	**Ida**	**Ida/ Vuelta**	**Dias**
08:00	10:15	11/09/2002	31/12/2002	7.05€	13.15€	L M X J V
08:00	10:15	11/09/2002	31/12/2002	7.05€	13.15€	S D
09:00	11:20	11/09/2002	31/12/2002	7.05€	13.15€	L M X J V
12:00	14:20	11/09/2002	31/12/2002	7.05€	13.15€	L M X J V
12:00	14:15	11/09/2002	31/12/2002	7.05€	13.15€	S D
16:00	18:15	11/09/2002	31/12/2002	7.05€	13.15€	L M X J V
16:00	18:25	11/09/2002	31/12/2002	7.05€	13.15€	S
19:00	21:25	11/06/2002	31/12/2002	7.05€	13.15€	L M X J V
20:00	22:25	11/06/2002	31/12/2002	7.05€	13.15€	L M X J V
21:00	23:10	15/09/2002	30/06/2002	7.05€	13.15€	D
21:30	23:55	03/07/2002	31/12/2002	7.05€	13.15€	L M X J V S D

Time: Leaving and arriving	Dates: From To	Cost of a single and return	Days

Origen: DENIA					Destino: ALICANTE	
H. Salida	**H. Llegada**	**Desde**	**Hasta**	**Ida**	**Ida/ Vuelta**	**Dias**
06:45	08:50	11/09/2000	31/12/2002	5.6€	10.4€	L M X J V S
07:45	09:50	11/09/2000	31/12/2002	5.6€	10.4€	L M X J V
10:15	12:30	11/09/2000	31/12/2002	5.6€	10.4€	L M X J V
10:15	12:30	11/09/2000	31/12/2002	5.6€	10.4€	S D
11:20	13:20	11/09/2000	31/12/2002	5.6€	10.4€	L M X J V
14:15	16:20	11/09/2000	31/12/2002	5.6€	10.4€	S D
14:20	16:20	11/09/2000	31/12/2002	5.6€	10.4€	L M X J V
18:15	20:30	11/09/2000	31/12/2002	5.6€	10.4€	L M X J V
18:25	20:00	11/09/2000	31/12/2002	5.6€	10.4€	S
18:25	20:15	11/09/2000	31/12/2002	5.6€	10.4€	D
23:10	00:30	15/09/2001	30/06/2002	5.6€	10.4€	D

Figure 12. Interpreting a timetable

'Una Talgo billete para Barcelona, por favor. No fumador.'

'¿Ida?'

'No, ida y vuelta, por favor.'

TELEPHONE COMMUNICATIONS

Telefónica, the Spanish telecommunications company, has improved its service since the state monopoly was removed in 1998. It is a well-respected company within the European marketplace in which it operates. Its shares are widely traded in stock exchanges and no portfolio is complete without a holding in this blue-chip company.

Dialling

There are no city codes in Spain, each area having its own two or three digit code number – e.g. Madrid 91, Barcelona 93, Malaga 95 and Valencia 96, Asturias 98 – followed by a seven- or six-digit number.

Charges

Charges are among the highest in Europe but have been reducing steadily in recent years. Telephone charges include the cost of the calls, line rental, telephone and other equipment rental less the cost of any subscriber discount packages. There are six tariffs: metropolitan (local and Internet), provincial, inter-provincial, international, mobiles and 90 numbers (*rastro*). Peak tariff hours are from 0800 to 1700 hours from Monday to Friday and 0800 to 1400 on Saturdays. Normal tariff hours are from 1700 to 2200, Monday to Friday. Reduced tariff hours are from 2200 to 0800 Monday to Friday, 1400 to 2400 on Saturdays, all day on Sundays and national public holidays. There are numerous discount packages aimed at moving demand from peak periods and conversely additional charges for operator connected calls and other services.

The *factura* (bill) is sent every two months allowing 20 days for payment. It is itemised providing a listing per number called (except for metropolitan and Internet calls) with the date and time, duration, number of units and the charge. Bills can be paid in cash at certain banks but more usually via a bank account, which is advisable for non-resident homeowners as it ensures the phone line is not disconnected for non-payment.

Directories

Telephone directories are published per province. The first few pages contain useful information:

◆ emergency and important local numbers for police, ambulance, fire brigade, etc.;

◆ Telefónica numbers and the services offered;

◆ national and international codes;

◆ tariffs and explanation of the *factura* (bill).

The main section is an alphabetical list of subscribers listed under their town or village and not alphabetically for the whole of a province. A new subscriber is automatically included in the next edition of the telephone directory unless choosing to have an unlisted number.

Public phones

As well as public telephones (*cabinas*), which allow international direct dialling, there are usually payphones in bars, cafés and restaurants. Phone cards can be bought at news-stands and tobacconists. There are also public telephone offices called *locutorios*, containing multiple phone booths and a fax service.

Mobiles

The sales of mobile telephones have rocketed everywhere including Spain. Both analogue and digital networks cover all the major population centres, although sparsely populated areas are not served by either landline or mobile systems. The main players are Telefónica with their brand Movistar and Vodafone.

POSTAL COMMUNICATIONS

The yellow signs outside each post office best identify *Correos* the national postal service of Spain. Yellow is also the colour of mail vans, delivery scooters and mailboxes. Mail to and from Europe is automatically sent airmail. Delivery of mail in Spain is within three or four days from the UK. But it can be slow in large cities, rural communities and on some urbanisations that have only a twice-weekly service.

Try to avoid the inside of some Spanish post offices. They can be small and dark with long, slow-moving queues. Go to the *tabac* for stamps. The cost of a stamp is the same for all EU countries although the pricing structure for various envelope sizes seems unnecessarily complex. Spaniards still distrust what was once a diabolical service and send their mail by certified or registered post or seek a receipt for each item sent.

'Diez sellors, por favor.'
'¿Para España?'
'Si.'
'Y diez para Europa tambien.'

The post office offers a range of services. Registered or express mail, parcel post, redirection, private boxes and banking are all available. Letters are delivered to a household door or, American style, to a driveway gate. On urbanisations all the post boxes are grouped together besides a focal point such as the swimming pool. It is necessary to go to the post office to collect parcels or registered mail when personal identification may be required.

All is not well with the Spanish postal system. Delays and strikes are common. 'Mail Boxes Etc.' a US company, has a number of offices in Spain. Although still dependent on the services of *Correos* it operates independently for overnight international parcel delivery through companies such as UPS and FedEx. It also offers a mailbox service, shipping and packing, fax and photocopying. It sells office supplies and stamps. This enlightened company is refreshing to deal with but its activities are restricted by the protectionism offered to the state postal system.

GETTING THE NAME AND ADDRESS CORRECT

Spanish names are important – a mother's maiden name is added to the end of a full name, women do not change their name when they marry, and the formal prefix of *Don* or *Doña* is introduced at the start of a name.

Señor Don John Frederick Smith King is simply Mr John Smith with a middle name Frederick and a mother's maiden name King. He is married to Señora Doña Maria Dolores Sanchez Vicario. Conchita Smith Sanchez is their daughter.

An accurate address is important:

Sr Smith
Calle Madrid 27, 2
03189 Orihuela Costa
Alicante

Translated this means:

Name		Mr Smith
Number	Street Floor	27 Madrid St, 2nd Floor
Post Code	Town	03189 Orihuela Costa
Province		Alicante

The zip code 03189 has 03 as the province number and 189 the post office number.

TV, RADIO, NEWSPAPERS AND BOOKS

Television

Digital TV now dominates this media. Most ex pats wish to tune into English-language programmes. These can be found on Spanish, BBC and Sky digital systems beamed through a satellite dish. Urbanisations offer a better selection of English, French, German, Scandinavian and Spanish channels through an underground cable system.

There are a number of Spanish television stations but Spanish television is dominated by pay-as-you-view programming of films and football, together with the standard news, documentaries, music, soaps and old films.

Radio

A mention should be made of radio. Spanish FM stations are available by the dozen, all with music and endless chatter. *Onda-Cero* covering both the Costa del Sol and the Costa Blanca is the best but more interestingly, however, are the popular UK-based FM stations available by satellite. These stations are received by digital receiver or by separate FM cable.

Newspapers and books

These are of great interest. Local, national and international, daily, weekly and monthly, Spanish and English, expensive, cheap and free publications – all clog the newsstands. Spanish daily newspapers are mainly middle class. *El País* (*The Country*) and *El Mundo* (*The World*) have lots of pages aimed at the serious reader and are cracking good value for money. At the bottom end of the Spanish daily press the content is devoted solely to football.

All the European daily newspapers are available. They are printed in Spain but cost three times more than the national edition. Weekend newspapers also have some sections missing. The best read for the ex-pat are the locally printed English-language weekly newspapers. They are a good blend of national and local news, lots of gossip, information and adverts.

Popular English books are difficult to find but large and small English bookshops do exist. Second-hand exchange libraries exist too. However, a wide choice of books is quickly available via the Internet with Amazon providing an excellent service from both the UK and USA.

DID YOU KNOW?
Cuentame

A Spanish TV soap, which dares to look back at Spain's most sensitive years, is pulling in more than six million viewers each Thursday. The groundbreaking series *Cuentame Como Paso* is the story of a family living through the Franco regime at the end of the 1960s. Most people thought Spain's skeletons were best left in the cupboard but the success of the show proves that Spain has grown up enough to look back at its painful times and it no longer wants American soaps about doctors, policemen and real-life shows like *Gran Hermano*.

Like many people the series follows the fortunes of a family who have left their pueblo behind to make a life in the city. It is a time of rapid development and change. A Seat 600 was a car of dreams and people could be admonished for kissing in public. Republicans at heart the family believe in leaving politics to the politicians and working hard to achieve success and happiness.

SUMMARY

- Driving in Spain is still a pleasure but care is required in large cities, rural towns and on some dangerous motorways.

- While purchasing a new car is similar in all European countries, the market for second-hand ex-rental cars is different.

- There is a lot of complex administration with motoring. Where possible put it in the hands of a *gestor*.

- Travelling by train has benefits if covering long distances. Slow trains are not all bad and if you are not in a hurry the savings are considerable. Special trains can be fun.

- Spain's telephones are on a par with most European countries.

- The postal service is by and large satisfactory but make sure you get the address correct.

- Television is now digital, radio now all FM, English newspapers, printed in Madrid, and easily available though expensive.

Appendix 1
Gibraltar – A Rock in a Hard Place

Gibraltar is at the southern tip of Spain. It belongs to the UK but Spain, with some justification, wants it back. Britain, experienced and pragmatic in these situations, says, 'let the people decide.' The people, rather like their brothers and sisters on the Falkland Islands, prefer the regime they know rather than the uncertainty of a new one. And so it goes on. But pressure mounts, as both Spain and the UK are partners in Europe. The semi-European status of Gibraltar needs to be resolved. Governments vacillate. The ordinary Spaniard has been surveyed many times:

◆ 49% want Gibraltar integrated into Spain;
◆ 41% are not against Gibraltar achieving independence;
◆ only 6% support joint sovereignty status.

Gibraltar has an image of typically English pubs, fish and chips shops, British retail outlets, together with tax-free electrical and liquor outlets. The tourist attractions still play patriotic songs such as 'Land of Hope and Glory'. But things are changing. Britain's fortress is dominant no more, and young Gibraltarian's are now born in a community where the working partnership is no longer with Her Majesty's Armed Forces, but with leading European and international financial companies.

The Rock has moved on from servicing the former vast armies and fleets of Britain's Empire to learning skills which exploit its unique position inside the EU. Gibraltar remains outside the EU VAT structure and the Customs Union. It has EU jurisdiction in its own right for sovereign and fiscal purposes, but is subject to most EU directives and rights. This complex legislative structure will probably alter yet again when Spain and Britain eventually resolve their differences.

The trans-shipment of vehicles, offshore betting, e-commerce and industries that use qualified company status complement a finance centre dominated by banking, self-holding investment structures, trusts and insurance work. This is the new central pillar of work opportunity and the economy of the Rock.

The future? E-land, naturally. Five years ago two computer enthusiasts took the plunge and set up Gibraltar's first Internet provider – Gibnet. Scepticism was promptly followed by addiction, and soon the most senior people were avid e-mailers. Then came Victor Chandler and Ladbrokes with offshore betting, its success causing a change to the UK betting tax laws.

The most exciting move in recent years has been a memorandum of understanding signed between the

Gibraltar government and a specialist in complex web hosting, increasingly described as net-sourcing. The project depends on their ability to provide high-quality, secure and reliable management for websites. The base for this international hub of predominantly financial sites is at Lathbury Barracks, formerly the heart of the British Army. The 80 million euro project will place the Rock at the heart of a worldwide industry expected to grow five-fold over the next few years.

It would be wrong to simply gloss over the Rock's imperial past. The minute you arrive on the bizarre airstrip between the Rock and Spain you can see its strategic importance. Four kilometres long and one kilometre wide, it is a towering impregnable fortress on one side of the narrow strait that bottles the Mediterranean into an inland sea. It also has a huge harbour.

Both sides of the strait are political anomalies. Ceuta is a Spanish possession in Morocco. Gibraltar is a British possession in Spain ceded in perpetuity by King Phillip V in 1713. It has survived many attempts to recover it, including Franco's closure of the border for 16 years.

It is as a colossus of British naval history that Gibraltar is famed. Nelson sailed from here in 1805. In the nineteenth century it was the staging point for a far-flung Empire and it played an important part in both World Wars, especially as an anti-submarine base. In 1942 the existing tunnels were extended to contain generators, a telephone exchange, food stores, a water desalination plant, a bakery and a hospital.

Today most visitors to the Rock are on duty-free shopping sprees but there is plenty to fascinate the historically curious including the 32 miles of tunnels open to the public. Other visitors include migrating birds. They cross to and fro from Africa to Europe over a strip of land a few kilometres wide with Gibraltar to the east and Tarifa to the west. Migration takes place all year round but the key periods are spring for northward movement and autumn for southward movement.

Watching the migration is a highly organised process with extensive viewing points at Mirador del Estrecha near Tarifa, Punta Secteta near Algeciras, the Nature Reserve and the observatory at Jews Gate on the Rock.

Small birds fly beating their wings furiously. Large birds tend to soar and glide constantly seeking thermals and avoiding long stretches of water. This effectively means that twice per year it is possible to view the common migrants such as storks, eagles, vultures and buzzards soaring over the Rock.

Appendix 2
The British Embassy and
Consulate – what do they do?

The British Embassy has overall responsibility for the representation and promotion of the UK in Spain. The consular section provides services for British citizens in Spain and visas for those who require them to travel to the UK. The British Consulate General is in Madrid and is the issuing authority for all UK passports and visas in Spain. Other British Consulates in Spain can issue emergency passports, valid only for a one-way journey to the UK.

Application forms for passports and visas are available by post or to personal callers, or can be downloaded from their website. The site also offers information on subjects ranging from timeshares to victims of crime and child abduction as well as a range of travel information.

The Madrid Consulate also registers the births and deaths of British citizens resident in or visiting, Spain.

The Consulate can:

◆ issue emergency passports;

- contact friends and relatives to ask them to help with money and tickets;

- tell you how to transfer money;

- in an emergency, they can cash a sterling cheque up to £100 if supported by a valid banker's card;

- as a last resort give a loan to get you back to the UK;

- help with local lawyers, interpreters and doctors.

The Consulate cannot:

- intervene in court cases;

- get you out of prison;

- give legal advice or start court proceedings;

- investigate a crime;

- pay hotel, legal, medical or any other bills;

- pay travel costs except in special circumstances;

- find you somewhere to live, a job or a work permit;

- formally help if you have dual nationality and are in the country of your second nationality.

The main web site is www.ukinspain.com. It is well worth a visit as it demonstrates links with the British Council and the British Tourist Board. How your country is presented abroad is also interesting. A list of locations and telephone numbers of the Embassy and its Consulates are given below.

British Embassy, Madrid	Tel: 917008200
Alicante	Tel: 965216190
Barcelona	Tel: 93 3666200
Bilbao	Tel: 944157600
Cádiz	Tel: 956264479
Ibiza	Tel: 971301818
Las Palmas	Tel: 928262508
Madrid	Tel: 913085201
Málaga	Tel: 952352300
Menorca	Tel: 971363373
Palma	Tel: 971712445
Santa Cruz	Tel: 922286863
Santander	Tel: 942220000
Seville	See Málaga
Vigo	Tel: 986437133

Appendix 3
The Spanish Constitution –
Extracts

Following the death of Franco and the re-emergence of democracy on 31 October 1978 the Spanish Parliament adopted a new written Constitution. It received the approval of the Spanish people in a referendum held on 6 December 1978 and became law when signed by King Juan Carlos on 27 December 1978.

The rights and obligations of all citizens of Spain are set out in considerable detail in 46 articles. It specifically states that all foreigners will enjoy all the rights guaranteed by the Constitution. Viewed 25 years later the contents look very basic for a modern western European country, but in the aftermath of Franco they are the words of democracy.

In addition to the fundamental rights of equality before the law, of free speech and religious, ideological and cultural freedom, there are five Articles of particular interest, which can be summarised as follows.

♦ The dignity of the individual, free development of the personality, respect for the law and for the rights of others is declared to be fundamental. The law in conformity with the Universal Declaration of Human Rights and such other treaties will protect these rights and freedoms and international agreements as may be ratified by Spain (Art. 10).

♦ No one shall be tortured, chastised or submitted to inhuman or degrading treatment. The death penalty will be abolished, except under military law in time of war (Art. 15).

♦ No one can be deprived of his liberty except in the circumstances and in the manner laid down by law. Preventive detention shall last only for so long as may be strictly necessary to elucidate the facts of a case, and in all cases a person must be released or brought before a court within 72 hours. Anyone kept in custody must be informed immediately – and in a manner he can understand – of his rights and the reason for his detention. He is not obliged to make any statement and is entitled to the assistance of a lawyer in all judicial and police enquiries. The law accepts the principle of Habeas Corpus (Art. 17).

♦ A man is entitled as of right to privacy for himself and his family, and without his consent his home cannot be entered or searched, except under a judicial warrant or when a serious crime has been committed (Art. 18).

♦ Everyone has the right of access to the courts, to be defended by a lawyer, to be informed of any charges made against him and to have the protection of a public hearing without undue delay. He can bring evidence in his defence, refuse to make any statement, which might incriminate him, and is presumed innocent until proved guilty (Art. 24).

Appendix 4
Income and Expenditure Checklist

	Before retirement	After retirement
Income		
Regular earnings		
Bonuses		
Overtime		
Commission		
Interest (bank, investments)		
Investment income		
Spare time earnings		
Other income		
Company pensions		
Private pensions		
Disability pension		
War pension		
State pensions		
Total		
Outgoings		
National Insurance Contributions		

Pension contributions
Income tax
Social or sports club fees
Other subscriptions
Mortgage repayments
Interest on loans
Loan or hire purchase
   repayments
Credit card repayments
Insurance premiums
Local council tax
Water rates
Rent
Telephone/postage
Gas
Electricity
Other fuel or heating
Food, grocery and household items
Newspapers and magazines
Business travel
Private travel
Eating out and entertainment
Car running costs
Holidays, hobbies and leisure
Home, gardening, decorating
Furniture renewal
Washing machine maintenance
Savings
Clothing
Private medical cover
Cigarettes, confectionery and alcohol
Total

Appendix 5
The Best of Spain

Five cities to visit

- Alicante   A fine industrial, commercial and tourist city
- Barcelona   It rivals Madrid – bustling, colourful, and full of vitality
- Granada   Home to the rich heritage left by the Moors
- Madrid   The capital, worthy of its title
- Seville   Orange trees line its streets and river

Five places of historic interest

- Córdoba   The home of more than just bull-fighting
- Gibraltar   A legacy of imperial power
- Ronda   Sits on top of a massive rocky outcrop
- Salamanca   A university town
- Santiago de Compostela   Its towering cathedral has welcomed pilgrims for centuries

Five tourist hot spots

- Benidorm   Something for everyone
- Ibiza   Night and morning party life

- Mallorca   It has to be done – the top holiday island
- Playas de las Americas   Tenerife's modern, cheerful, sun, sea and sand location
- Torremolinos   Tired and past its best

Five restful locations

- Cullera   A river, a wide beach, but only known to the Valencianos
- Marbella   Where the rich and famous come to play
- Port de Soller   The French influence in Mallorca
- Puerto Morgan   Unique planning in Gran Canaria
- San Sebastian   Set in its own wide bay

Five mountain retreats

- Ainsa   A gateway to the Pyrenees
- Alcoi   In the heart of the Costa Blanca's walking region
- Competa   Set in high rounded hills close to Málaga
- Pollensa   A base for exploring Mallorca's rocky west coast
- Potes   Set in an amphitheatre of the Picos

Five places off the beaten track

- Arenas de Cabrales   Try the local black pudding
- Cuenca   See the overhanging houses
- Coruña   Exposed to the Atlantic at the northwest tip of Spain
- Oliva   The best beach and camp sites in Spain.

◆ Ruidera   A line of lakes formed by a rift in
                 the Meseta

Five places to treat with caution

◆ Extremadura   An area of Spain remote from the
                 modern world
◆ Fuengirola   Demolish it
◆ Loret del Mar Give this Blackpool with sun a miss
◆ Orihuela Costa In summer it's wall to wall with
                 people
◆ Playas del Inglés Flats, hotels and neon developed in
                 Gran Canaria in the 50s

Appendix 6
Saying Hello

The most common Spanish greeting is *Hola* (Hello) and *Buenos dias/tardes/noches* (Good morning/afternoon/evening). It is a normal politeness to use these terms together when entering a shop or if passing someone on the street.

If you are introduced to someone you have a choice of expressions, a choice that hinges on the appropriate level of familiarity. If you are introduced to an unknown adult it is best to err on the side of formality, shake hands and say something simple such as *Encantado* or *Con mucho gusto* (Pleased or Delighted).

It is common to hear Spaniards saying *¿Hola, como esta usted?* (Hello, how are you?) The standard response is *Bien gracias* (Good, thank you). When introduced to a young person such greetings may suggest unnecessary formality. *Hola* or *¿Qué ta?* (How are you?) is a more normal greeting.

The rules about greeting with a kiss on the cheek are somewhat ambiguous. The safest advice is to shake hands rather than kiss older women. It is usually quite acceptable for younger people, when they are presented to each other, to kiss on the cheeks. It should be noted that this 'kiss' is the slightest of actions. Quite often lips do not even touch the skin but rather the people lean forward and touch cheek to cheek.

Appendix 7
Classic Spanish Recipes

Gazpacho Soup (serves 6)
2 cloves garlic
A pinch of cumin
1 kg ripe tomatoes or 840 g canned tomatoes
2 medium onions
½ large cucumber
2 large green peppers
3 thick slices white bread
5 tablespoons olive oil
3 teaspoons salt
6 tablespoons wine vinegar
1 litre water

Peel the garlic and pound to a paste with the cumin in a bowl or mortar. Drop the tomatoes into boiling water for 1 minute, remove then peel and coarsely chop them with the onions and cucumber. Remove and discard the seeds from the peppers and chop the flesh. Soak the bread in cold water for about 30 seconds, then squeeze out the excess moisture.

Place three-quarters of the chopped vegetables in a blender with the garlic paste, bread and oil, and reduce to a purée, or chop finely by hand, then pour into a bowl, stir in the salt, vinegar and water and chill thoroughly. Very finely chop the remaining vegetables and place in small bowls. Serve the gazpacho very cold in deep soup bowls or cups.

Each diner chooses vegetables from the small bowls.

Valencian Paella (Serves 6)

1 large chicken, about 1.5 kg or the same weight of chicken pieces
3 teaspoons salt
1 kg fresh peas, or 225 g frozen peas
225 g flat green beans, fresh or frozen, or French beans
1 medium tomato
1 clove garlic
5 tablespoons olive oil
1 litre water
1 teaspoon ground paprika
3 saffron strands
12 canned, drained cooked snails
450 g short-grain rice
1 lemon, cut into wedges to garnish

Cut the chicken into 15 pieces and sprinkle with salt. Shell the peas if fresh. Trim the beans and cut into 5–7 cm pieces. Drop the tomato into boiling water for 1 minute, remove and peel. Peel and chop the garlic. Heat the oil in a paella pan or in a large, heavy frying pan. Sauté the chicken pieces for 5 minutes, then add the garlic and tomato and sauté for 2 minutes. Add the peas and beans and sauté for another 2 minutes. Add the water and paprika and bring to the boil. Add the saffron strands and snails. Lower the heat and simmer for 20 minutes. Add about a cupful of boiling water or enough to replace that which has evaporated, raise the heat until the water is boiling rapidly and then stir in the rice. Boil for 2 minutes, lower the heat and simmer gently for about 12 to 15 minutes or until the rice is tender and dry. Remove from the heat, but leave on the hot stove for 5 minutes, then garnish with wedges of lemon and serve straight from the pan. Each diner squeezes the juice from the lemon wedges over the paella.

Sangria
The juice from 2 lemons
The juice from 4 oranges
A little cinnamon
1 litre good red wine
½ litre lemonade

Mix the ingredients, chill. Add fruit to taste such as oranges, peaches, grapes and lemons.

Appendix 8
Public Holidays

1 January	New Year's Day
6 January	King's Day
19 March	St Joseph's Day
March/April	Good Friday or Easter Sunday
1 May	Labour Day
25 July	St James Day
15 August	Assumption of the Virgin
12 October	National Day
1 November	All Saints Day
6 December	Constitution Day
8 December	Immaculate Conception
25 December	Christmas Day

The central government allows 14 days paid public holidays per year. Twelve of these days are given above. Additionally, each region celebrates its own holiday with most towns and villages also having their own carnival and fiesta days. If a holiday falls on a Tuesday or Thursday, shops and offices may be closed on the intervening Monday or Friday making it a long weekend.

Northern Europeans find the frequency of Spanish holidays confusing and ignore all but the main religious holidays.

Appendix 9
Clothing and Shoe Sizes

Female shoe sizes

Spanish	36	37	38	39	40	41
British	3	4	5	6	7	8

Male shoe sizes

Spanish	39	40	41	42	43	44	45
British	6	7	7.5	8	9	10	11

Female dress sizes

Spanish	40	42	44	46	48	50	52
British	8	10	12	14	16	18	20

Male suits

Spanish size	44	46	48	50	52	54	56
British inches	34	36	38	40	42	44	46

Male shirts

Spanish cm	36	38	39	41	42	43	44
British inches	14	15	15.5	16	16.5	17	17.5

Should a purchase need altering it is still common for a shop to offer the services of a seamstress free. The alteration is completed within 24 hours. Men's trousers are still sold in one, very long, leg length.

Appendix 10
The Communities of Spain and their Provinces

The provinces of Spain are grouped into 17 autonomous Communities. Asturias is a *Principado*, Murcia is a *Región*, Navarra is a *Comunidad Foral* while all the rest are classified as *Comunidades*. The name, address, the first two digits of the provincial postcode and the old provincial letters used on vehicle number plates are shown below.

Northern Spain

Comunidad Galicia, Palacio de Rojoy, 15705 Santiago de Compostela

Galicia			
	15	La Coruña	C
	27	Lugo	LU
	32	Ourense	OR
	36	Pontevedra	PO

Principado de Asturias, Calle Suarez de la Riva, 33071 Oviedo

Asturias	33	Asturias	O

Comunidad Cantabria, Calle Casimiro Sainz 4, 39003 Santander

Cantabria	39	Cantabria	S

Comunidad Pals Vasco, Palacio de Ajuna-Enea, 01007 Vitoria

Basque	01	Alava	VI
	20	Guipuzcoa	SS
	48	Vizcaya	BI

Comunidad Floral de Navarra, 31002 Pamplona

| Navarra | 31 | Navarra | NA |

Comunidad La Rioja, Calle General Vara del Rey 3, 26071, Logrono

| La Rioja | 26 | La Rioja | LO |

Eastern Spain

Comunidad Cataluña, Plaza de San Jaime, 08002 Barcelona

Catalonia	08	Barcelona	BA
	25	Lleida	L
	17	Girona	GE
	43	Tarragona	T

Comunidad Aragon, Diputación de Aragon, Paseo Maria Agustin 36, 50071 Zaragoza

Aragon	22	Huesca	HU
	44	Teruel	TE
	50	Zaragoza	Z

Comunidad Valencia, Palau de la Generalitat, 46003 Valencia

Valencia	03	Alicante	A
	46	Valencia	V
	12	Castellon	CS

Región de Murcia, Palacio de San Esteban, Calle Acisco Diaz , 30071 Murcia

Murcia	30 Murcia	MU

Central Spain

Comunidad Madrid, Puerta del Sol 7, 28013 Madrid

Madrid	28 Madrid	M

Comunidad Castilla La Mancha, Palacio de Fuensalida Plaza de Conde 2, 45002 Toledo

Castilla la Mancha	02 Albacete	AB
	13 Ciudad Real	CR
	16 Cuenca	CE
	19 Guadalajara	GU
	45 Toledo	TO

Comunidad Extremadura, Calle Jose Fernandez Lopez 18, 06800 Merida

Extremadura	06 Babajoz	BA
	10 Caceres	CC

Comunidad Castilla y León, Plaza de Castilla y León, 47006 Valladolid

Castilla y León	05 Avila	AV
	09 Burgos	BU
	24 León	LE
	34 Palencia	P
	37 Salamanca	SA
	40 Segovia	SG
	42 Soria	SO
	47 Valladolid	VA
	49 Zamora	ZA

Southern Spain

Comunidad Andalucia, Palacio de San Telmo, Avda de Roma, 41071, Seville

Andalucia	04	Almeria	AL
	11	Cádiz	CA
	14	Córdoba	CO
	18	Granada	GR
	21	Huelva	H
	23	Jaen	J
	29	Málaga	MA
	41	Seville	SE

Islands

Comunidad las Islas Balaeres, Calle Marina 3, Consulado del Mar, 07012 Palma de Mallorca

Balearic Islands	07	Baleares	PM

Comunidad las Islas Canarias, Plaza 25 de Julio 1, 35004 Las Palmas de Gran Canaria

Canary Islands	35	Las Palmas	GC
	37	Tenerife	TF

Appendix 11
Useful Addresses

Accommodation – paradores, hotels and spas

Asociación de Termales	www.balnearios.org
Cuevas Perdo Antonio de Alarcon	www.travel-in-spain.com
Hotusa Hotels	www.hotusa.es
Husa Hotels	www.husa.es
Novotel	www.novotel.com
Paradores	www.paradores.es
Santos Hotels	www.h-santos.es
Sol Melia Hotels	www.solmelia.es
Tryp Hotels	www.tryp.es

News and information

BBC World Service	www.bbc.uk/worldservice
Stanford's (maps, guides and travel books)	www.stanfords.co.uk
Gibraltar Tourist Board	www.gibraltar.gi

Financial Planning

Blevins and Franks	www.blevinsfranks.com
Financial Services Authority	www.fsa.gov.uk

Independent Financial Advisor Promotion	www.ifap.org.uk

Employment

British Council	www.britishcouncil.es
British Executive Service Overseas	www.beso.org
Educational Visits and Exchanges	www.britishcouncil.org
Graduate jobs	www.prospects.ac.uk

Furniture removal

Britannia International Removals	www.britannia-movers.co.uk
Bishops Move	www.bishops-move.co.uk

Holiday home rental, exchange and timeshare

Internet sites	www.europropertysearch.com
	www.holidayhome.co.uk
	www.holidayrentals.co.uk
Intervac Home Exchange	www.intervac.co.uk
Timeshare Consumers Association	www.timeshare.org.uk

Interpreting

Simply Translating	www.lshl.com
Susan Bultitude, 03700 Javea	www.susanbultitude.com

Pets

Department of Environment (export of dogs and cats)	www.defra.gov.uk/animalh/ quarantine

Property sales

Atlas International	www.atlas-international.com
Masa International UK Ltd	www.masainter.com
Propertunities Ltd	www.propertunities.co.uk
Spanish private sales	www.loot.com
Spanish property portal	www.newhabitat.com
Taylor Woodrow	www.taywoodspain.co.uk

Retirement

Age Concern	www.ageconcern.org.uk
Occupational Pensions Registry	www.opra.co.uk
Pre Retirement Association	www.pra.uk.com
UK state pensions	www.dss.gov.uk

Taxation

Inland Revenue (former UK taxpayers now living abroad)
Fitzroy House, PO Box 46, Nottingham NG2 1BD

Internet	www.inlandrevenue.gov.uk

Travel and flights

British Airways Authority	www.baa.co.uk
Brittany Ferries (Plymouth to Santander)	www.brittanyferries.com
Easy Jet	www.easyjet.com
E-bookers	www.ebookers.com
Eurostar	www.eurostar.com
Eurotunnel	www.eurotunnel.com
Foreign Office Travel Advice	www.fco.gov.uk/travel

P & O (Portsmouth to
    Bilbao)   www.poportsmouth.com
Spanish railways   www.renfe.com

Appendix 12
Further Reading

CHAPTER 1

Living and Working in Spain (ECA International): demographics from the HSBC.

The New Spaniards, John Hooper (Penguin): an excellent work.

The Spanish Civil War, Gabriel Ranzato (Windrush): a century in focus.

The Spanish Tragedy, Raymond Carr (Phoenix): the civil war in perspective.

CHAPTER 2

Don Quixote, Miguel Cervantes (Penguin): a classic.

Federico Garcia Lorca – A Life, Ian Gibson (Faber & Faber): a definitive work.

Spain, Jan Morris (Faber & Faber): writing at its best.

Tales of the Alhambra, Washington Irvine (Sanchez): an American humorist in 1832.

CHAPTER 3

AA Essential Spanish Phrase Book (AA): common sense phrases.

Oxford Spanish starter dictionary (Oxford University Press).

Sueños World Spanish (BBC): multimedia course for beginner's Spanish.

Viva España (BBC): beginner's language course.

CHAPTER 4

Active Retirement (The Which? Guide): highly recommended.

Allied Dunbar Retirement Planning Handbook, David Bertram: (Financial Times).

Good Non Retirement Guide, Rosemary Brown (Kogan Page): updated annually.

How to Retire Abroad, Roger Jones (How To Books): a guide to a happy retirement abroad.

CHAPTER 5

Doing Business in Spain (Price Waterhouse): a business guide.

Getting a Job Abroad, Roger Jones: (How To Books): now in its fifth edition.

Teaching English Abroad, Susan Griffith (Vacation Work): getting a teaching job.

Teaching Abroad (AGCAS): more about teaching.

CHAPTER 6

Eyewitness Spain (Dorling Kindersley): the best travel guide.

Paisajes (Comunitat Valenciana): where to go.

Special Places to Stay, Alastair Sawday (ASP): a roof off the beaten track.

Which? Guide to Spain Consumers' Association: a well thought out book.

CHAPTER 7

Buying a House in Spain, David Hampshire (Survival): a jocular style.

Buying a Property in Spain, Harry King (How To Books): an easy-to-read guide.

Buying and Selling Your Home in Spain, Per Svensson (Longman): an older book.

The Spanish Property Guide, David Searl (Santana): a detailed legal approach.

CHAPTER 8

The British Council: publications and information on learning and cultural exchanges.

Higher Education in the EU, official publications of the EU (Kogan Page).

S*panish Courses for Foreigners in Spain*, Ministry of Education, Madrid.

Study Holidays, Central Bureau for Educational Visits and Exchanges.

CHAPTER 9

Culture Shock, Marie Louise Graff (Kuperard): a guide to Spanish customs and etiquettes.

Death in the Afternoon, Ernest Hemingway (Grafton): his famous look at bullfighting.

The Sun also Rises, Ernest Hemingway (Grafton): fiestas.

The Spanish Temper, V. S. Pritchett (Hogarth): interesting.

CHAPTER 10

Cooking in Spain, Janet Mendal (Santana): the essential cooking book for Spain.

Spanish Wines, Jan Read (Mitchell Beazley): a good wine guide.

Tapas and More Great Dishes from Spain, Janet Mendal (Santana): Spain's bar food.

The New Spain, John Radford (Mitchell Beazley): another well illustrated wine guide.

CHAPTER 11

Driving Over Lemons, Chris Stewart (Sort Of Books): a humorous optimist in Andalucia.

Land of Valencia, Comunitat Valenciana.

Spanish Lessons, Derek Lambert (Ebury): humour – beginning a new life in Spain.

Sunflower Landscapes (Sunflower Books): four walking guides

CHAPTER 12

A Guide to the Spanish Taxation System, (Henry Woods with Spence Clarke).

Fact sheets from the Money Management Council: easy to read guides.

Living in Spain, Bill Blevins and David Franks: financial affairs for residents.

You and the Law in Spain, David Searle: (Santana): detailed.

CHAPTER 13

Fact sheets from the *ayuntamiento*, in English, on Spanish procedures.

Health and Illness in Retirement, Anne Roberts (Ace Books): recommended.

Tell the Doctor, Calle El Moreral 3, 03792 Parcent, Alicante.

We Are in Hospital (Alicante University/Cam Bank): one for the bookshelf.

CHAPTER 14

Gastronomy (Comunitat Valenciana): a what to buy free guide.

Costa Blanca News: weekly English newspaper with a host of advertisements.

Sur in English: as above for the Costa del Sol.

World Food: Spain (Lonely Planet): buying fun food.

CHAPTER 15

Internet Rough Guide, Angus Kennedy (Rough Guides): to keep in touch with home.

Master Windows XP (Maran Graphics): we all need this one.

The Guardian Weekly (Guardian Publications): sent to your new home.

The Weekly Telegraph (Telegraph Publications): also by post.

Index